Faith

FOR THE
JOURNEY

COMPILED, EDITED & ILLUSTRATED BY

DAVID LIVERETT

Faith

FOR THE
JOURNEY

DAVID LIVERETT

FOREWORD BY CHRISTIE SMITH STEPHENS

Chinaberry House
P. O. Box 505
Anderson, Indiana 46015-0505
www.2Lights.com

Cover: Painting by Norman Rockwell
Printed by permission of the
Norman Rockwell Family Trust
Copyright © 1951 the
Norman Rockwell Family Trust

ISBN 0-9632180-1-8
Printed in the United States of America

Unless otherwise noted, scripture quotations are taken
from the HOLY BIBLE, NEW INTERNATIONAL
VERSION®. NIV®.
Copyright © 1973, 1978, 1984 International
Bible Society.
Used by permission of Zondervan Bible Publishers.

Dedication

Charles Nelson Moore was my pastor during the "turning point" years of my teens. This book is dedicated to him with love and friendship.

Foreword

Granddaddy Smith loved his grandchildren, all fifteen of us. He was handsome, a tall man with beautiful white hair. I remember his large arms around me and feeling very safe in his care. He and Grandmama helped start the Austinville Church of God in Decatur, Alabama, a long time ago. Granddaddy, Brother Smith as he was known to David Liverett and other folks in our congregation, sang bass in the choir. We can still see him standing in the back row of the choir loft near the beautiful painting of the waterfall by William Bixler. Aunt Masinah remembers when William Bixler came to the church and painted that land/waterscape while the congregation watched. We can still hear Granddaddy, Brother Smith, singing his favorite hymn, *The Kingdom of Peace* by Brother Barney Warren. The fourth verse ends, *"O what rapture and bliss are awaiting, When our faith shall be lost in the sight!"*

Granddaddy's faith became sight-in-part many times during his eighty-five years on earth. His faith became full-sight-eternal when he went home in June of 1975. While he was here he did his best to walk with God albeit his faith was a real life, human thing. I think he knew that no matter where he was, God was walking with him. He had his doubts especially after Grandmama died. Doubts that quietly remained even when we sang *"all our doubts are passed away."* Sometimes he was sad and even despairing but he kept on singing.

Granddaddy liked to tease his grandchildren a little. He used to take his finger and draw a mark on our shoulders or arms. "I'm putting a question mark on you," he'd say. "I'm putting a question mark on you." I always experienced that question mark as a mark of my granddaddy's love for me and as a mark of his sense of humor, a sense of humor that was a gift of God. As years have passed I have come to treasure that question mark bestowed upon me by a loving grandfather, a question mark symbolizing his faith when it was not yet sight, a question mark granting me permission to question, to wonder, to doubt, to seek on my journey of faith not yet sight.

Or as the father who asked Jesus to heal his son put it, *"I believe; help my unbelief."* I realize that others may interpret that question mark upon me in quite different ways and they could be right.

Robin Morgan, writer, shared the poet Rilke's philosophy "to have patience with everything unresolved in your heart and to try to love the questions themselves." The theologian, Paul Tillich, defines faith not as being without doubt or question but as "being grasped by ultimate concern." He said, I believe, that our questions are evidence of our faith. That made sense to me. I am so grasped. As the song in the movie, *Yentl,* asks, "Why have a mind if not to wonder why?" And are not our minds gifts of God? The philosopher Cornel West encourages critical thinking and invites us to engage in the "spirituality of doubting." Optimism and hope are radically different, he says. Hope is not the result of optimism but is resurrected from the experience of despair. Faith, I am persuaded, is a dynamic process of belief and unbelief, of seeking the truth that sets us free, of integrating the question marks, the periods, the exclamation marks, the ellipses and the dashes into the whole story of who we are as the children of God. We journey on until that day when we will sing with Brother Warren, my granddaddy and the hosts of saints and angels of *"our faith now lost in the sight!"*

See now the lovely churches drawn by artist David Liverett, churches and drawings witnessing to the faith of individuals and congregations, to the faithfulness of God in all times, *"scenes of grandness before us."* Hear now the testimonies of the faithful telling the stories of their journeys of faith, *"the themes that are sweet to our memories, the joys we cannot express, treasures that gladden our being..."*

"O, what rapture...O, what bliss..."
Peace,
Christie Smith Stephens
Thanksgiving, 2001

Table of Contents

Introduction

ittle country churches have always had a special place in my heart. Originally, the little country church was the art theme for this book. The emphasis changed after September 11, 2001. When I heard what St. Paul's Chapel had done in relieving the suffering at Ground Zero, I felt that I should broaden my focus. In the beginning I wanted to bring some honor to a forgotten institution. I observed two things during my research that altered my vision. The first was noted when in search of a particular church that I remembered, I discovered to my surprise that it had been razed. The other observation was the many changes that have been made to churches to meet the needs of today. Some of the changes were minor such as removal of chimneys and the additions of handicap ramps and enclosed entrances to accommodate a narthex and restrooms. Still other churches have completely engulfed the original building or sold the facility and built a modern efficient structure. Sadly, some of these buildings did not find a congregation and are left in ruins.

Drawing churches for this book was not a big leap from what I have done most of my life. As far back as I can remember, I have drawn in church. I grew up in a small

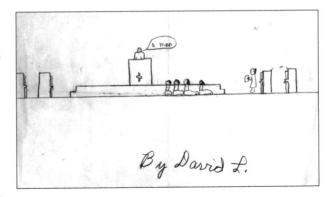

church in Austinville, Alabama, with an average attendance at the time of a hundred. It seems that I was always drawing people in church or studying a huge oil painting that William Bixby had painted behind the pulpit. After my mother and father died in the early 1990s, I discovered that my mother had saved an early drawing of mine. It shows the people at the altar and the minister in the pulpit saying, "A man."

I have always had a love for art and architecture. My brother and I would draw houses on Sunday afternoon instead of taking a nap. Being four and a half years younger than he, my goal was to draw as well as he did. After high school I worked for almost three years as a draftsman. In college my part-time job was working as a commercial artist for a large publishing house, Warner Press in Anderson, Indiana.

After my book, *When Hope Shines Through,* was published in 2001, I thought that little country churches would be a natural art theme for my next work. Lighthouses and churches have much in common. Many churches have tall spires much like the lighthouses and each are noted for having bells. The bells of the churches are rung to welcome the people to the sanctuary. Lighthouse bells are sounded to warn the people to stay at bay. Both churches and lighthouses have rescuing legacies.

The cover of a book is very important. Norman Rockwell has had an influence on me since I first saw *The Saturday Evening Post.* I thought the painting, *Saying Grace,* would make an ideal cover for my book if I could get copyright approval. After a series of telephone calls, I made contact with Tom Rockwell and worked out the clearance to use this famous painting. In the painting, *Saying Grace,* the scene shows a grandmother with her grandson sharing her faith, generation to generation.

When I asked my friends if they would help with this project, some had had experiences similar to mine but others were nurtured in large congregations. The opportunity was given for each writer to furnish a photograph of their church for me to draw. Some could not locate any photographs of their churches so I have included a few of my favorite architectural styles. An attempt was made to write a brief statement about the history of each church. In some cases this was not possible.

I thank all the writers for their contributions and I hope that the people who touched their lives will touch yours. I thank the people who found photographs and stories about churches for their assistance. I thank those who read the manuscript and offered suggestions. I especially thank my wife, Avis, and my friend and assistant, Tamara Burrell, whose creativity and skills have been vital to the publication of this book. I will be forever grateful to my family and to the congregations that have shaped my life.

Let me be clear. I know the difference between the real church and the church building. I learned this important lesson in Sunday school.

I remember and I imagine that you do too. Lock your fingers together and say with me: "Here's the church. Here's the steeple. Open the doors and see all the people!"

Here's the church! See all the people!

David Liverett
Anderson, Indiana
March 14, 2002

Austinville Church of God Groundbreaking of New Sanctuary - 1962

Front row: Emma Smith, Florence Garrett, Sam Germany (pastor)
Second row: Carly Linderman, Hal Garrett, Dick Dean, Howard Smith, Clifford Poole, Lonny Petty and Buck Martin.
Third row: Marguerite Liverett, Una Russell, Mina Dell Skinner, Dorothy Garrett, Olivia Hall, Bonnie Poole, Annie Garrett, Lucy Williams, Maude Dean, Lizzie Hamilton, *unidentified, unidentified,* David Liverett, Jimmy Dean and Kenneth Smith

"Therefore confess your sins to one another, and pray for one another...
The prayer of the righteous is powerful and effective."
—James 5:16

Are You Available?

Robert H. Reardon

My spiritual journey began early on. I am in my mother's lap. It is Sunday morning in the Park Place Church of God and my father is in the middle of his sermon. I am making my dear mother as miserable as possible, thrashing about, making loud angry comments and kicking the back of Sister Sherwood's seat. It took only a moment for my father to leave the children of Israel pressing on toward the promised land, close his Bible, walk down from the platform, scoop me up in his arms and carry me, with a thousand pairs of eyes following, into a place of reckoning which was painful for me, but

Robert Reardon as a preschooler

I think it was pleasing for Sister Sherwood. I am told that a holy silence fell on the congregation until father finished his business and returned to seat me in a different state of mind. He then returned to the pulpit to pick up Moses and the quest of the promised land.

My spiritual pilgrimage is not a story of a rebel far from home leading a dissolute life eating in a pig pen. It was my good fortune to be born in a strong, loving family. My sins had to do with playing marbles for keeps, an occasional ten cent shot in a drugstore slot machine, or misspending school money on candy or a racy magazine like *Uncle Billy's Whizbang*. Such sins were soon discovered, brought to my attention, discipline was administered and prayers for forgiveness offered to God at the family altar. I bowed at this altar many times. But I did learn that dishonesty and bad

Old Park Place Church of God (1906) - Anderson, Indiana

On September 20, 1906, one hundred and seventy workers from the Gospel Trumpet Company came to Anderson, Indiana. The following Sunday these workers met in a rented building at the corner of Ninth and Central Streets. The Trumpet Workers Home with a chapel was completed in November. By 1916 the church started a building fund. Several people thought the logical site for this new building was a vegetable garden at the corner of Eighth Street and what now is College Drive.

The building, completed by November, 1917, was in the familiar Akron style with slated floors and had the chancel located in the corner. The sanctuary, with a wrap-around balcony, brought together eleven hundred persons.

In the early 1960s, after the new Park Place Church was completed, this building housed the Anderson College Music Department and chapel met here twice a week until a fire distroyed it in 1967.

Robert Reardon as a preschooler

conduct had their price and that there was a line beyond which I was not to go, which I learned first as a child in church. Until I was well into my teens, I tended to think of being a Christian in terms of conduct.

It was during my years at Anderson College in which I was blessed with teachers that pressed me to think of my life as a gift and the possibility that God had a plan for me in mind. After a great deal of wandering about trying to decide exactly what that was, I was getting nowhere. In my senior year, late one night, I heard God's voice. It was a voice that one may hear in a moment of

truth, deep in his mind and heart. He said He was not ready to deal with the details...only my response to the question "Are you available?" This was the definitive moment in my spiritual journey. I answered "yes." Through the years I have come back to this place of surrender many times. It is an altar which has brought me to opportunities of service I never dreamed of, resources beyond imagination, and the fulfillment of God's promise to walk beside us as friend and guide.

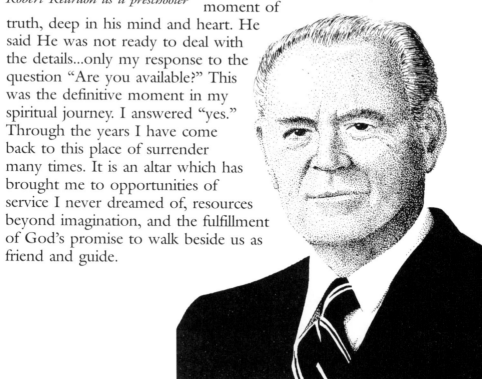

Robert H. Reardon

"...Isaiah says, 'Lord, who has believed your message?' Consequently, faith comes from hearing the message, and the message is heard through the word of Christ."
—Romans 10:16-17

Early Religious Experiences

T. Franklin Miller

In the summer of 1910 in southwest Missouri, my father was a tenant farmer for Dale Oldham's grandfather. Mr. Oldham brought his son, W. H. Oldham, grandson, Dale, and J. T. Wilson for a three-week open-air preaching mission held on his farm. There was one convert—my mother. I was a baby in her arms, so I have no memories of those Missouri experiences. Dale did; he was eight years old. When I was three, we moved to Cedar Rapids, Iowa, where I spent the next fifteen years.

When I was about five years old, my father was converted under the preaching of visiting preacher, J. T. Wilson; that night I do remember. From that time on our family regularly had family worship and attended every event in our little store-front Church of God. I recall a later move to a modest new church building. One Sunday School teacher I remember above all others—Mrs. Hanisch, who nurtured her *children* and was helpful to me in my early religious experiences.

Visiting evangelists, many of them, always stirred my heart, and in those childhood days I often bowed at an altar for prayer. My parents were devout and faithful Christians, and our church and its activities were always central in our family life—far ahead of school or community affairs. I was about eleven years old when I made a conscious and full commitment to God, and was baptized soon after. The *terrible teens* were especially difficult for me. I was sensitive and conscientious, in a church and family with rigid and tight-laced standards of behavior. I struggled with guilt over what I now know should not have been a problem to a young Christian, but I was in faith and understanding, constantly dealing with the rigid legalism of the church and, often, my family. I was not really comfortable with

Malden Church of God (1926) - *Malden, Massachusetts*

In the 1930s, the Church of God developed a church-wide plan for planting new congregations in five major metropolitan areas. Everett, near Boston, was one of these. Financial assistance was supplied through the newly created Board of Church Extension and Home Missions. In 1926, the church began in Everett, Massachusetts, with Dr. Earl Martin as the first pastor, followed by Steele Smith in 1935. When T. Franklin and Gertie Miller came to pastor the church in Everett in 1937, a move was made to Malden. In 1942, a building was constructed.

Other early pastors included Lilla M. Simmons, Charles Diezel, Albert Donaldson, Ivan E. Watts, L. W. Lewis, Byron Chew and Gilbert Stafford.

any of my classmates at school, many of whom I admired and esteemed. The very word *worldly* caused me untold agony of conscience.

More maturing religious experiences came in my late teens, largely influenced by two deeply committed Christian high school teachers and two of the many pastors who shepherded our church.

In my twenties my faith grew rapidly. I was in and out of Anderson College during the depression years and I moved from the stern and irrational legalism to a more mature faith. God surely led me into *green pastures* as I became better acquainted with outstanding Christian persons. I began preaching much too soon, and was helped beyond measure by a long parade of great pastors for whom I preached as a VERY YOUNG evangelist. In the

T. Franklin Miller

years since, God has led me into rich and wonderful experiences of faith, and is still doing so. I am in unpayable debt to scores of Christians who have patiently encouraged me, and I thank God so often for those wise, kind, patient mentors, and for the daily leading of the Holy Spirit.

*"Better is one day in your courts than a thousand elsewhere; I would rather be a
doorkeeper in the house of my God than dwell in the tents of the wicked."*
—Psalm 84:10

A Legacy of Faith

Avis Kleis Liverett

My grandma, Grace Fleser, was a saint. To be sure,
when I was growing up I didn't know she was a
saint. To me she was a jolly, good-natured, loving
grandmother who made the very best sugar cookies in the whole
world. Known to her eighteen grandchildren as "Grandma Fleser's
Cookies," the cookies have not been duplicated exactly since
Grandma ceased baking them in the sixties. Many have tried, but in
these health conscious days none of us has the desire to purchase and
use her secret ingredient—lard! And in our busy schedules filled with
short cuts and timesavers none of us has the time to roll and cut the
cookies as she did. I can remember watching, fascinated, as she cut,
lifted and flipped a lovely round shape from the cookie cutter, a
drinking glass, to her left hand and onto the baking sheet in the
twinkling of an eye. The cookies were well seasoned, not only with
her loving touch, but also with a generous amount of nutmeg, my
grandfather's favorite spice. There was always a shaker of nutmeg on
the dining table along with the salt and pepper!

When we made our yearly summer visit to my grandparents'
home, there were certain traditions that I expected to participate in
each year. Every morning after breakfast, Grandma, market basket on
her arm, would head down to the local general store. I loved to go
along on these trips down the street and around the corner. I would
help find the groceries Grandma needed and place them in her
basket—no shopping carts in that little store back then. A trip to the
store and on down the street to the post office for the mail and
news were important events in my grandma's daily life. Even more
significant in Grandma's life were trips to her church. Every Sunday,
rain or shine or snow, she was present for services. Usually, she
taught a Sunday school class and sang in the choir. The walk was
even farther than to the store and post office, the church being near
the edge of town. But Grandma didn't make that journey only for

Burnips Methodist Church (ca. 1868) - *Burnips, Michigan*

Somewhere in the vicinity of 1868 there was a church in Burnips Corners, Michigan. The church was called the "Church of God." This group of twelve people held meetings in the schoolhouse. Their own building was construced in 1873. As many members moved, or passed away, the volume of this church decreased so greatly that their services were finally discontinued in the mid-1880s. The buidling changed hands at that time to become the house of worship for the Methodists.

In 1900, the citizens of Burnips built a new brick building which was to serve the congregation for about sixty-five years. It was located across the street from the old church between a school and a pickle-packing factory. In 1964, the brick building was abandoned in favor of a new structure. The old church bell was retained and hung in a memorial to Mrs. Grace Fleser. The mortgage of $23,500 was paid in full just ten years later. A joyful service of dedication was held on November 10, 1974.

Sunday services. There was an evening prayer meeting each week and sometimes a week of revival services. When the other church in town held a revival she attended those services also. The Methodists and *The Pilgrims* (Pilgrim Holiness Church) might talk about each other on porches, in backyards or kitchens, but during each other's revivals they joined forces to pray for the unsaved of the community.

Grandma's faith, as was expressed in her faithful attendance, always included her growing family. My mother had memories of the time when her father became a Christian. His visits to the town saloon ended, as well as his and Grandma's involvement in Odd Fellows and Rebekahs. At that time, Grandpa Fleser began going to services at the little German Methodist church about two miles out in the country that his relatives attended. Since he had no wagon and never owned a car, he had no way to transport his wife and children to that country church. He received criticism from the townspeople, but my mother believed my grandma was just thankful that he was going to church. Grandma and all eight of her children made many a journey to that little church at the edge of town.

Not only did Grandma and Grandpa set an example for their children and grandchildren by faithful church attendance, but also in family devotions. By the time I had reached the age of remembrance, devotions took place at the breakfast table. Often on warm summer mornings I was awakened by my grandpa's booming voice as he and Grandma knelt in front of their chairs on the hard kitchen floor and lifted their petitions to the Lord above. I can remember waiting at the bottom of the stairs hidden by the stairway door for the prayers to end, so I could make a trip through the kitchen to the bathroom!

Over the years Grandma fulfilled many roles in the little Methodist Church of Burnips, Michigan. For many years she had the job of custodian. During the week she made sure the building was clean. She would arrive early for services to open the door, make sure the furnace was heating in winter and to ring the bell. I remember being at Grandma's house and hearing the peal of the bell across the town and knowing that we had fifteen minutes to get to church on time. Usually, as we walked in the door, we would see her pulling the bell rope to signal the start of the service.

Grandpa and Grandma went to be with the Lord in 1968 and 1969 respectively. Their memorial services were held in that little church in Burnips and they in turn were buried in the town cemetery.

Many years after my childhood a new church building was erected and the old one torn down. When I attended as an adult, I still recognized many of the people, but one by one they slipped away, including my grandparents. The bell from the old church was saved and a few years later a memorial shelter was constructed to house it. The bell in its new setting was dedicated in memory of my grandmother. Many family and community members gathered for that service which honored Grandma's many years of servanthood in that tiny town.

Today when David and I are nearby, we not only stop to visit the graves of my parents and grandparents, but we also always visit *Grandma's Bell*. The inscription on the support beam under the bell reads "Dedicated to the memory of Grace Fleser, doorkeeper in the house of her Lord."

I believe that faith does not always come to us as an abrupt about-face turning point in our lives. Sometimes it is there from our earliest memories like a secure presence surrounding and enveloping us and keeping us safe. That presence was there in my home, as I grew up, providing a love for me other than the love of my parents. Little seed thoughts were dropped along the way from stories read and told by my mother and numerous Sunday school teachers. In due time the seeds germinated, took root and grew into a mature faith, an entity from which to draw strength for daily living.

My grandmother's faith was passed to each of her eight children. My mother, named Faith, claimed that faith for her own at an early age. Eventually she had the opportunity to nurture her own daughter in the faith she had seen lived out in a tiny old church in a very little town. That my son was raised in a home where he was taught to know and love the Lord was due in part to my grandmother's life of faith. When I hear my grandson, now two, state emphatically at the end of a prayer "...mem," I know that Grandma's faith has stretched across five generations. It truly is a legacy of faith.

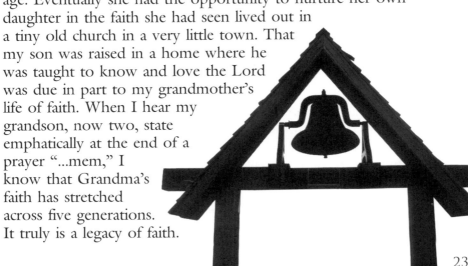

"Fight the good fight of the faith. Take hold of the eternal life to which you are called when you made your good confession in the presence of many witnesses."
—1 Timothy 6:12

Testimony

Herschell D. Rice

The twelfth of twelve children of a poor farming family, I was born in a small farmhouse in Montague County, Texas, in 1915. By the time I had reached age seven, several of my older brothers and sisters had left the farm, and my father realized we couldn't make it any longer in Texas. The family moved to western Oklahoma, settling on a farm outside Elk City. Between helping with chores and picking cotton, I went every day to a one-room country school. Life was difficult for our family in the first years of the Great Depression. We were held together with the firm discipline of my father and the faith and prayers of my God-fearing mother.

Shortly after being converted, I felt God's call upon me to preach. In those days, the *call* was enough. So I just started preaching at about age seventeen. Most of my early sermons were before a captive congregation...the cows and pigs behind the barn. By the time I was twenty years of age, I was a full-time evangelist, had just gotten married to Freda Madden, was only known in Oklahoma, and came into contact with a man who would change my life.

At the time, F. G. Smith was the foremost theologian of the Church of God. He traveled around the country lecturing and holding revival meetings. At a camp meeting he was conducting at Clinton, Oklahoma, I met him for the first time. Several of the older pastors told him about a young evangelist they felt had great potential. He heard me preach, and apparently saw something in me that sparked an interest in becoming my mentor. Why he took a liking to me I will never know. But he advised me to get some formal training at Anderson College and Theological Seminary in Anderson, Indiana. I had never been very far from home, and Indiana seemed a world away, but if F. G. Smith thought I needed to go to college to learn how to preach, then I would do it.

The Oklahoma brethren ordained me at age twenty-two, and the

Mount Olive Chapel - Episcopal (1857) - *Pineville, Louisiana*

*The oldest structure was completed in 1857. It served as a barracks
for Union soldiers at one time during the Civil War.*

Herschell D. Rice –1938

next year (1938) Freda and I and my brother Hillery and his wife Pauline headed for Indiana to enroll at Anderson College. F. G. Smith was pastor of the Church of God in Akron, Ohio, one of the strongest churches in the movement. Shortly after I reached Anderson he asked if I would hold a revival in his church. I was astounded. He was the most outstanding preacher in the Church of God and he was asking me, a country preacher recently arrived from Oklahoma, to fill his pulpit. After each service we would talk for hours about preaching, and he would carefully and in great detail critique each sermon. Our styles were different; he was more of a teacher and I was definitely evangelistic. But I knew I could learn something from anyone, and listening to him evaluate my preaching was like sitting at the feet of a master. He felt the future of the Church of God would be in the hands of young men like myself who believed something and said it. I certainly believed it and was never afraid to say it. Of all the influences in my life, F. G. Smith was the greatest. I am what I became largely due to his influence and his mentoring me at the formative period of my ministry.

A few months later...it must have been 1939...he called and asked me to come again to hold another revival. This was unprecedented; two revivals in F. G. Smith's church in the same year! In the fall of 1940 it appeared as if we would have to return to Oklahoma because we had no money for tuition. As we were preparing to leave Anderson, I received a call from Dean Russell Olt to come to his office. He told me that someone had paid my tuition in full and that I should never ask who it was. To this day I do not know the identity of that anonymous donor. I have wondered if F. G. Smith was in some way involved.

After the attack on Pearl Harbor in 1941, F. G.'s son Galen and I marched to the local recruiting office and registered for the draft together. We stayed in his and Birdie's home several times, and our friendship continued until his death.

In looking back, without a doubt my ministry turned around when I met F. G. Smith. There must have been many other young men with as much or more potential as I had. But the difference was in the directing and prodding and encouragement given me by this great man. In my early days in the Church of God ministry, I preached many times at Anderson Camp Meeting. Very few young men were given that privilege in those days, and F. G. Smith was responsible for my being included in the program a total of twenty-four times. Each time he continued in his role as mentor. He pushed, and I began to get calls from all over the country to come and preach. I've held four hundred revivals and preached in every camp meeting the Church of God ever had.

F. G. Smith has been gone for many years, but his memory continues. Because of his influence, I too have felt inspired and called to mentor and coach young preachers. It is they who have now taken over for me just as I took F. G. Smith's place. Under my ministry, teaching, and mentoring have come Gerald Marvel, Morris Williams, Norman Patton, Jay Barber, Dean Schield, Loren Myers, Ken Wilson, Bill Bryant, Tim Poldrugo, and Steve Elnhorn...and like a pebble thrown in the water, our influence will go on forever and ever and ever.

F. G. Smith

*"I will sing of the LORD'S great love forever; with my mouth
I will make your faithfulness known through all generations."*
—Psalm 89:1

The Wildwood

Eugene W. Newberry

There are almost two billion Christians in the world and most of them do not and did not attend little white-painted churches. I did, in my youth, and I still give a look, a double look, when I drive past that *church in the valley by the wildwood.* And I hum the tune. The sweet sentiment and gratitude are often more than I can contain. There were Clell Porter, my Sunday school teacher and Charles Cartmill, my pastor and Bill Livingston and Charles Sparks, my best friends. For about ten years we worshipped, studied, sang, took trips, had parties *(no dancing)* and played softball. This church was my life. The Baptists usually beat us in softball.

There was a good deal of judgment in the preaching I heard and it was frightening. But basically the leaders talked about Christ, His love and forgiveness. We were invited to a journey of faith, a fellowship of sharing and witness. My six-year-old sister, Betty Jane, died after a week's illness with polio. Two weeks later I knelt at the altar. As a junior high boy that little white church became my refuge from fear and doubt, my station of grace and hope, my journey with Christ. It determined my education, my vocation, my friends, my marriage and family, and ultimately my destiny. I feel nothing but thanksgiving.

My colleague, Dr. John W. V. Smith, closed his ministry with an impressive book, *I Will Build My Church*. His wisdom is a cut above the personal experience I've described. He defines the biblical base for Jesus' counsel, and the ingredients in the church experience. Christ calls us to a great heritage, a great fellowship and a great responsibility. I need both a creditable experience and theology to go with it.

We just called David Markle to be our pastor. He looks and sounds wonderful. Yesterday the sermon, the organ, the choir, the scripture, the prayers and the communion service brought peace and joy to my soul. Wednesday night we started *Body Life* for the autumn and winter. It is fun, food, fellowship and lessons for two hundred or so of us. Whether in that little white church or this big colonial edifice, I find nourishment for my soul and a roadmap for my journey.

Primitive Baptist Church (1827)
Cades Cove, Tennessee

"...The only thing that counts is faith expressing itself through love."
–Galatians 5:6

The Country Church

Margaret Jones Smith

No Man's Land, later to be known as the Panhandle of Oklahoma, was settled by homesteaders claiming the prairie for a new home. Life was not easy, but as soon as they had built houses for their families, they built churches and schools. There are not many hills on the prairie, but the site for the church was a hill that overlooked the community. The church was a beacon set on a hill.

More than a hundred people came to the dedication of the Bethel Church in Beaver County, Oklahoma. Farmers came from miles around to sing, to pray and to hear the scriptures expounded. Revival meetings were held every fall after the crops were in. Prayer was a time of calling on the Lord from their knees and the altar bench was the place of commitment.

Music was the language of the people. There were family singing groups that added to the church services, the men's quartet that sang together for thirty years and a ladies trio that traveled to conventions and camp meetings.

The church was also the place for celebrating family events, such as weddings and funerals. Neighbors shared their joys and heartaches. Frequently there was dinner on the grounds and a singing in the afternoon. Christmas programs were special events with music and drama. The program ended with the distribution of Christmas bags of ribbon candy, chocolate cremes, walnuts and big red apples for the children.

John and I were married in the Bethel Church in June, 1942. We stood before the altar in that white church on the hill and pledged our love to each other "until death do us part." God was especially near as we shared our commitment to each other before our families and friends. The church on the hill had been an influence in determining our values and our mission. On our thirty-fifth

Bethel Baptist Church (ca. 1920) – *Beaver County, Oklahoma*

In 1923, a revival was held in the Bethel Baptist Church and the Methodist Church, the Baptist Church, the Presbyterian Church and the Mennonite Church organized a congregation known as Bethel Church of God. In 1924, this new congregation built a church building two and a half miles southeast of the Bethel Baptist Church. This new building was patterned after the Baptist Church. The building and congregation are still an active part of the community.

Margaret
Smith

anniversary we returned to that church. No one was there to be our witnesses, but we stood before that altar again and repeated our vows and knew that the values and mission found in that church still directed our lives.

The Bethel Church still stands on the hill. In my imagination I still hear the singing and the *amens.* There is no steeple or bell tower to call the people to worship, but on Sunday mornings the neighbors gather to worship as their parents and grandparents did before them.

"...From now on all generations will call me blessed, for the Mighty One has done great things for me—holy is his name."
—Luke 1:48-49

Connections

Arthur M. Kelly

My faith grows through living in relationship with God, with friendships, and within my family. Faith and family—such rich words, full, deep, and wide with meaning. Without beginning, stretching far back into the dim recesses of time, and, of course, far out into God's future. The roots of my faith in God grow deep—through family—in two soils: the lovely green lands of England and the Isle of Man through my father and the rich red dirt of Oklahoma through my mother. My living faith is enriched by these connections.

In 1994, I headed across the Irish Sea to the Isle of Man. A lovely green jewel, set in the Irish Sea, eighteen miles wide and thirty-three miles long from which my father's family migrated. My journal records that visit to the family church—vital to my faith journey.

"The next morning we headed out in search of the family church, Kirk Bradden, and found it, actually two kirks, old and new, and found records but no graves. The churches are beautiful—one very old and very simple, surrounded by an ancient graveyard where, I'm sure, some of our family must lie, covered by beautiful, pungent, oniony flowers.

"The old Kirk Bradden has been here for a very long time—at least the site. A Synod was held there in the late 13th century; other dates indicate that this was a Christian site as far back as the Christian Viking kings of the 900s. It is very simple, plain, even austere. With a Sunday school in the back. A three-tiered pulpit; each with a lectern. No stained-glass. Markers and memory stones on the walls. Pews with kneeling benches and three family booths. It is still in use.

"We wandered around in the graveyard hoping to come upon a Kelly; but it is a very old yard, very full, and many of the stones are weathered beyond reading. Rubbings might have revealed some, but

Old Kirk Bradden (1774) - *Isle of Man in the Irish Sea*

Old Kirk Bradden was rebuilt in 1774. The ecclesiastical parish of Bradden in the Isle of Man is about six miles long and two miles wide, and lies to the south and west of the town of Douglas, the capital of the island, which is on the east coast.

The parish includes the Anagh Coar, Ballaughton and Farmhill suburbs of Douglas, as well as the villages of Union Mills and Kewaigue within a rural area stretching from Douglas Head to Mount Rule. According to the 1996 Isle of Man Census, the population of the parish is 6,521.

we hadn't the time for that. It is a moving experience to wander among such stones. I felt at home; I felt connected. The British Isles are full of stones—full of death, I guess, one might say, but not in a negative sense; life has been in this place a very, very long time and there is a direct connection between the monoliths of Stonehenge, the stones of Old Kirk Bradden, and me. People laboring, making a living, loving and hating, raising children, marrying off those children and dying—all within some understanding of a God who makes it all possible—however hard and quixotic that God *(or gods)* might seem.

"And I am walking among them—the stones and roots of our family, walking the Isle which produced us. But my stones will be elsewhere."

In ways beyond reckoning, I sense that the faithful pilgrimage I travel today began in this church and on this island. I am connected here, and such connections define my faith, and matter to me in ways I cannot yet explain, however deeply I feel them. But they do matter: They have formed me.

"I press on toward the goal to win the prize for which
God has called me heavenward in Christ Jesus."
—Philippians 3:14

Catching the Vision

R. Eugene Sterner

It was several months after my parents and I had
become Christians that Forbes Kilgore, a nearby farmer
and a member of the Church of God in Callensburg,
Pennsylvania, drove his model A Ford across the rough country
roads to our farm home to share some of his convictions about the
nature of the church and Christian unity. He brought his well-worn
Bible. I can still see him tracing with his rough, gnarled fingers, the
various passages describing the first century Christian fellowship. He
spoke of the church as all Christian people in a fellowship of love
committed to the cause of Christ, and of the division that hindered
that cause. I caught a vision that calm summer evening that is with
me yet after seventy-four years.

At Mr. Kilgore's invitation we started attending that small church,
though it had no pastor. I was fifteen years old, going to high school
in Callensburg. My earliest experiences with the Callensburg
congregation were life-changing. My father worked at night but
I went to prayer meeting on Wednesday nights where five older
people met together, the Kilgores, the Linamens, and Mrs. Davis.
I was the only young person in the church and those dear people
took me to their hearts. They prayed, too, that *this truth* would be
known throughout the earth. Little did I know that one day
I would have a small part in the answer to that prayer.

I graduated from high school when I was almost eighteen. The
Great Depression had come and the only place for me was there on
the farm, but my mind and heart dwelt upon what I should be
doing with my life. Increasingly God's call gripped me. I wanted to
go to college but I had neither job nor money. In the fall of 1934,
I took the plunge and entered Anderson College. With only minimal
training I became pastor of the small congregation in Ellwood City,
Pennsylvania. There were three other student pastorates, then other
assignments including work in the general agencies of the Church of

First Church of God (1909) - *Callensburg, Pennsylvania*

In 1909, a pioneer minister of the Church of God, John H. Rupert and his wife Hattie arranged to have a van constructed and to secure a tent equipped with chairs and other things to do summer gospel work. Upon completion of the van, Rev. Rupert was led by the Lord to come to Callensburg and lead a meeting. Three were saved and began meeting in the Texters' home for worship until the next summer when the Ruperts would return.

In 1911, they returned and many were saved. The congregation in Callensburg began to grow through these tent meetings. The Ruperts stayed through the winter and plans were made to build a Saints' Chapel. In 1912, the building was completed and the church continued to grow. In 1920, Nora Hunter visited and organized the missionary society.

God, located in Anderson, Indiana.

In 1967, when I was fifty-five years old, I was asked to be Director of the Radio and Television Commission and Speaker on the Christian Brotherhood Hour. Suddenly I was actually speaking to millions of people around the world. The program was on some four hundred stations in the United States plus some of the most powerful stations elsewhere in the world, ten and fifteen times more powerful than are allowed by law in the USA. What a privilege! Mail came

R. Eugene Sterner

from many other countries and I did a great deal of teaching and counseling by mail, until retirement in 1977.

Many, many times I have thought of the dear people in Callensburg. I have been richly blessed with many opportunities across denominational lines and have worked with some I called *spiritual giants*. Though I haven't been to Callensburg for many years I still think of that church with gratitude and love. At this writing, I am eighty-nine years old. As I look back on seventy-four years of Christian pilgrimage and sixty-seven years in the ministry, I am so deeply grateful for the undeserved blessings of the Lord.

"Be on your guard; stand firm in the faith; ...be strong. Do everything in love."
—1 Corinthians 16:13

The Little Chapel That Could

Christie Smith Stephens

Houses of Faith have their journeys, their stories, their testimonies, their witness to the faithfulness of God. Sometimes little chapels have big, true tales to be told by children who remember the storm and receive its gift.

Stan, my husband Stan, remembers the return of the Ice Age to the Niagara River in 1955. He was eleven almost twelve that winter, a child of this wild, powerful landscape. It was a different time. He and his friends used to descend and ascend the gorge, the Devil's Hole, carved out by the thundering Niagara Falls through centuries. They explored and absorbed this fierce, beautiful terrain to which they were born. Inside him still is the gift of belonging to this particular waterscape. He misses it as one misses a beloved parent no longer here, yet indelibly imprinted upon one's soul.

The Niagara River has frozen over many winters. It is not uncommon for there to be an ice bridge between the USA and Canada; not uncommon though illegal for people to walk the ice between these two friendly countries. But the ice of 1955 was uncommon. It was in the words of a child, "HUGE!" Ice coming through Lake Erie from the upper lakes lumbered over the falls filling the gorge for fourteen miles to Youngstown, New York, and Niagara-on-the-Lake, Canada. It was a sight to behold. Stan's dad would drive the family along the gorge to Youngstown so that they could see the massive ice, formed, gathered and increasing there. As the old holiday song says, "the traffic was terrific." The ice jammed the gorge and became a real threat to life along the river. The Army Corps of Engineers set off dynamite charges trying to dislodge it but the ice was immovable. They decided they would just have to wait for the thaw and for nature to take its course.

When the first warmth came, the ice began to crack and soon to move with a mighty force. It changed life along the river forever, they

Our Lady of Sorrows Chapel (1913)
Stella Niagara, New York

Stella Niagra Convent and School was founded in 1908. Mother Leonarda had always wanted to build a chapel in honor of the Sorrowful Mother. Brother Joseph Stamen, S.J. who was also a contractor, was aware of this. He had in his employ a Mr. Heusinger who was ill with a diabetic condition. One day Brother Stamen told Mr. Heusinger that he should go to Stella and build this chapel in honor of the Sorrowful Mother, and that in return he should petition Our Lady for a cure. (The little building was a partial ruin on the riverbank.) It was said that from the day Mr. Heusinger started to build the chapel his health steadily improved and on September 15, the Feast of the Sorrowful Mother, when the chapel was finally finished, he found himself cured. Mr. Heusinger charged the sisters nothing for his labor; they supplied only the materials. The chapel remains to this day, a testament to God's healing power.

say. Bergs of titanic proportion stabbed each other as they fought for space. The cracking could be heard for miles. The ice moved down river toward Lake Ontario spreading onto the lower fields clearing the land in its path. Trees, cottages, and cabins fell prey to the frozen fury that would not be denied. This glacier with a mind of its own terrified residents who scurried to save what could be saved.

Up on a hill between Lewiston and Youngstown, New York, stood and still stands the motherhouse and school of Stella Niagara. The sisters looked down on the meadow below where the Our Lady of Sorrows Chapel sat near the river. They could no longer see their prayer chapel. The ice had risen to obscure the view. They saw pieces of houses and willow limbs sticking out among the peaks of ice. It appeared that their little chapel had fallen victim to the substance from the lowest level of Dante's hell. Archangel Michael had lost this encounter with the archenemy. As the ice receded the miracle revealed. The tiny chapel had been protected as the nuns say by Mother Mary, sheltered in the arms of God. A thirty-foot wall of ice had surrounded this sanctuary and saved it. Not even a window was shattered.

This is a survival story the sisters and others who remember the return of the Ice Age in 1955 love to tell. In 1999, Stan and I and our friends, Patsy and Wayne Gordon, walked down the hill from Stella Niagara to the little chapel. We opened the doors and saw the beautiful artwork on the walls and ceiling telling the story of protection and salvation. The small steeple houses a bell and lifts the cross. Not far away is a shrine proclaiming, "My Peace I Give Unto You." Four friends on a journey of friendship of long standing felt the *hedge* of protection around us, the peace that passes understanding. Lest I give in to a cheap grace, a too easy belief, or get too simplistic in trying to tell the story, it should be noted that the riverside bar also survived the ice. Perhaps, this additional message is that God does not reduce to the story I can tell.

Stan remembers the storm, the thundering assault of nature, the loss, the remnant that remains. Inside him is this childhood experience and the story of the water, the falls, deep gorges, abysses to descend and ascend, ice, warmth, melting, destruction and salvation. His interior, soul and spirit, landscape was formed by an exterior landscape once upon a time in the fiercely beautiful world of Niagara Falls. As Jon Levenson says, "Geography is simply a visible form of theology."

"Humble yourselves, therefore, under God's mighty hand, that he may lift you up in due time. Cast all your anxiety on him because he cares for you."
—1 Peter 5:6-7

God Sent a Prayer

David L. Sebastian

sense of need is a gift. Only an empty vessel can be filled. But often pride and self-reliance keeps us from experiencing the empowering presence of the Holy Spirit. Scripture reminds us to *"Humble yourselves before the Lord, and he will lift you up." –James 4:10.*

Several years ago, I received word that my mother had been diagnosed with a brain tumor. As a result of the surgery she suffered a stroke. The surgeon requested that the family come home, for the prognosis for recovery was not good.

I secured a flight and flew across country. After having briefly visited my mother in the intensive care unit, I went to the chapel where I took a seat in the last pew of the chapel.

In the front of the chapel was a young girl. I discovered later she was a senior in high school. She prayed in an interesting manner. She would sing and then she would pray. She would pray and then sing. Reverently she would sing and pray. I sat quietly in the back of the chapel with my head bowed in prayer for my mother. There were words I wanted to speak to her even if they were only parting words.

Suddenly there was a hand on my shoulder. It was the young girl who had been praying in the front of the chapel. She asked, "Is everything okay?" She said empathetically, "The Holy Spirit impressed upon me to come back and pray for you. Is everything all right?"

Regretfully, my first response was "Yes, everything is just fine." After all, I am an ordained clergyman. I am the one who is supposed to ask such questions and pray such prayers. However, no sooner had I spoken those hollow words than I tried to catch and reclaim them for they were so untrue. I was not doing well and my heart was full of fear.

The young lady told me about her mother who was also in intensive care. She reported on the progress she was making against incredible odds. She told me how the Holy Spirit was so real to her

Mount Pleasant United Methodist Church
Kosciusko County, Indiana

and was helping her through this difficult time. Then she said, "If it is all right with you, I want to pray for you and your mother." She prayed. The prayer was one of the most powerfully moving prayers I had ever heard or experienced.

God answered the young girl's prayer. As a result we enjoyed my mother's presence for another five years before she went to be with the Lord. Five more years afforded me to speak the words I needed to say. Five more years my children were able to sit in Grandma's lap.

I never saw the young girl again, but her presence and prayer in that chapel allowed the Holy Spirit to minister to me in my time of need. To think I almost missed it because of pride and self-reliance.

Anderson University School of Theology (1961) - *Anderson, Indiana*

"Search me, O God, and know my heart; test me and know my anxious thoughts."
—Psalm 139:23

The Search

Gibb E. Webber

May blessings be upon the head of Cadmus, the Phoenicians,
or whoever it was that invented books!
—Thomas Carlyle

From childhood, I have been an omnivorous reader. None of my family had graduated from high school, so I had no mentor to answer my many questions about life and the world. I grew up in an isolated rural environment with no close friends. Consequently, I turned to books as my mentors and companions. It should not, therefore, be surprising that the most significant guides on my spiritual quest should be books and their writers.

At the age of sixteen, shortly after my mother's death, I began attending church and soon made the expected visits to the altar to *get saved* and to *commit my life to Christ.* Since I could detect nothing that *happened* on these and subsequent altar trips, I decided that these phrases were, for me, only meaningless *church talk.* For approximately the next fifteen years, I maintained a comfortable relationship with the Christian community, enjoying the fellowship and even serving on church boards and committees.

I had never doubted God's existence, but, being of an analytical and skeptical mind set, I needed answers to the hard questions about Jesus Christ: Had He always co-existed with God? Was He born of a virgin? Was He literally resuscitated from death after His crucifixion? The answers I got from Christians I considered as platitudes: "You need to pray through until the answer comes." "Don't think; just trust and obey."

The questions continued to nag, however, and in my early thirties I left the institutional church to seek answers on my own, a dangerous but necessary choice for one who is convinced that his rational powers are a gift from God to be used to seek Him. Space does not permit me to detail my decade-long search here. Suffice it

St. Augustine Catholic Church
Natchitoches Parish, Louisiana

to say I eventually came upon a little book by John A. T. Robinson entitled *Honest to God*. Here I found not only a Christian but a bishop of the church who legitimized my questions. More importantly, Robinson directed me to the sermons of Paul Tillich, especially the collection entitled *The Shaking of the Foundations*. My reading of two of those sermons, *You Are Accepted* and *He Who Is the Christ*, marked a crucial turning point in my spiritual quest. For the first time, I understood what *getting saved* meant, and I was able to *commit my life to Christ*.

Have I found the answers to my Christological questions? No, I haven't. But I am content to live with the mystery, knowing that my life itself is *mystery cared for*. Albert Schweitzer has stated it profoundly: "But the truth is, it is not Jesus as historically known, but Jesus as spiritually arisen within men, who is significant for our time and can help it." I conclude, again in Schweitzer's words, with a most memorable description of the Christ:

"He comes to us as One unknown, without a name, as of old, by the lake-side. He came to those men who knew Him not. He speaks to us the same word: 'Follow thou Me!' and sets us to the tasks which He has to fulfill for our time. He commands. And to those who obey Him, whether they be wise or simple, He will reveal Himself in the toils, the conflicts, the sufferings which they shall pass through in His fellowship, and, as an ineffable mystery, they shall learn in their own experience who He is."

Amen and Amen!

"...I consider my life worth nothing to me, if only I may finish the race and complete the task the Lord Jesus has given me—the task of testifying to the gospel of God's grace."
—Acts 20:24

Sunday Morning Meeting Time

Gloria Sickal Gaither

If the journey of my life were a country road, the important landmarks along that road would be places of worship: the little white church with the pot-bellied stove in the center of the pews where I first heard about a land called Beulah, the village church where as a kid I listened to the old saints testify to the faithfulness of God through the years, the church by the river where I had my first date and the youth group would sing *Kum Ba Yah* around the campfire on the riverbank after Sunday night services. Along my journey is the church where I promised my sweetheart I'd be faithful 'til death do us part, and the place where we brought our first baby to be dedicated to God. And at one church by the road, I said goodbye to my precious father and, later, my mother and—because of those who came to share our grief—I knew I would not walk on alone.

So when the church bell rings this Sunday morning, I'll hear a whole chorus of bells in my heart, and I will go into the house of the Lord—full of gratitude for these landmarks along my path that have brought me to this Sunday morning meetin' time.

Burlington Church of God (1889) - *Burlington, Michigan*

The first meetings were held as early as 1889 in the home of
Henry Moser, outside of Burlington, Michigan. In 1893, a
chapel was built about three miles out of town. In 1911, the
church building was divided into sections and transported
into Burlington, it's present location, by bobsleds and teams
of horses. The building was then reassembled in it's original
form. Gloria Gaither's father, Lee Sickal, pastored the church
from 1948 to 1956.

"Be still, and know that I am God; I will be exalted among the nations..."
—Psalm: 46:10

Faith Comes in Many Sizes

Roscoe W. Snowden

My faith journey began as a brash teenager full of high hopes and absolutely sure that I could rely on the faith my parents exhibited and the church supported. I faced my expanding world of reality somewhere in my college studies preparing for a vocation in pastoral ministry. Gradually I became less and less sure of myself. In spite of my disturbing doubts and the awareness of the approaching time for graduation, I still felt the urge to be a minister. The decision was to seek a pastorate, keenly aware of my shortcomings, but willing to keep searching for answers. I needed a place to sort things out.

Seeking counsel from an older minister I admired and respected, I finally felt safe to ask, "Do you know of a church that is so far back in the mountains where I can be of some help and still not hurt them, and hopefully find some answers to my many questions?" He wrote me a few days before commencement time that such a church was needing a pastor in the mountainous region of western North Carolina in a community called Ivy Ridge. Without asking any questions and receiving none from the church, we accepted each other sight unseen, no trial sermons, no salary negotiations, no contracts. I just needed to show up the first Sunday of July, 1941.

I was not totally prepared for the cultural shock and environmental change that would be a big part of my life for the next several months. The church and the rustic cabin where I lived had no electricity, no running water except the clear mountain trout stream that had to be crossed on a footbridge to get to the cabin, and where I had to take my baths after darkness had settled over the valley. I learned to live without indoor plumbing, a telephone, paved roads and without street lights to push back the night. If I stayed too long at the home of some church member and night came on without a moon to assist me, I had to stumble through the darkness, because there were times when I could not see my hand in front of

Ivy Ridge First Church of God (1934) - *Mars Hill, North Carolina*

In the early 1930s, Henderson Norton had the vision of building a place of worship for the congregation. Worship services were being held in the Ivy Ridge School. Mr. Norton gave the land. He and Dempsie Blankenship walked about six miles across the mountains to rent saw-mill equipment. This equipment was hauled about eight miles to the site on a sled pulled by a team of six horses. Included was a steam engine and boiler. When the saw-mill was in operation, members furnished the logs. A foundation was dug out of the side of the hill. Wooden scrapes, (made from planks attached to bull tongue plows—pulled by horses) wheelbarrows, mattocks, shovels, and picks were used for the excavation. The foundation was oak logs hewn with a broad-axe and fastened with spike nails. Ceiling and walls consisted mostly of tongue and grooved chestnut and poplar. The inside was furnished with homemade wooden benches. Approximately six kerosene lanterns placed on shelves provided the lighting system.

me. I had no automobile, so I did what others of the community did, I walked. However, in this rural community and church family I found many people of faith willing to follow the teachings of Jesus and wonder of wonders they accepted me.

It was with some difficulty I told Brother Ramsey I had received a call to pastor a circuit of churches in the foothills of my home state, Kentucky. There he was, dressed in his often washed blue bib overalls and denim shirt, wearing heavy brogans suitable for walking the rocky roads or following a turning plow in a mountain field. The typical dark felt hat like all the men wore was turning nervously in his hand. He could not find the words he wanted to say but the quivering lips told me enough. The time for saying good-bye had come so we shook hands and I watched as big tears began to course down his cheeks.

I had not expected this and it never occurred to me that this man of few words really cared about me that much. I had gone to the mountains to find myself, a renewed faith, and willingness to believe in God. In this simple expression of tenderness, Brother Ramsey was helping me find that for which I was searching.

Two years later I decided to pursue post graduate studies at Morehead State Teacher's College. I was able to attend classes during the week and then drive to my churches each weekend. I was still searching and toyed with the idea of leaving the ministry and preparing to be a medical doctor. If I could be a family doctor this would be the best way to fulfill the need I had to help people. I enrolled in several courses that would assist me to get into a medical school if that became a real option.

Working in the lab one afternoon I scraped some rust spore from an oak leaf and placed it on a slide then pushed it under the lens of the microscope. As I brought it into focus I was surprised to see hundreds of red spores intricately formed and each one the exact copy of its neighbor. Then it hit me! How can this beauty and sameness of design be possible without some prior design and designer? Is all of this possible by chance, or is the hand of God at work here? It seemed a light was turned on, not very bright, but bright enough to cause me to reconsider the thought I was having regarding leaving the ministry and pursuing a career in medicine. This experience in the lab helped me to continue to carry out the responsibilities of pastor in a growing church.

While conducting Christian Education conferences, I met a mature missionary on furlough from India. He was most approachable and wise, and it was easy to share some of my questions regarding the willingness of the church to move beyond its provincialism and time-honored traditions. Again I questioned the wisdom of staying with a job when there were so few signs of change and acceptance of methodology more fitting for current times.

This gentle servant of God spoke kindly as he attempted to encourage me to stay with the church, pointing out that I was not alone in posing these questions and that he had met other young pastors facing similar problems; and stating further that one should stay with the church which would in time make changes. What he did not say was that I would also gain deeper understanding and faith and make changes in my way of thinking. I felt encouraged to stand firm in what I possessed, even if at times it was like a flickering candle.

Opportunities for service came at several levels following that conversation and I am glad I did not forsake the ministry. I learned that faith does not come in a "one size fits all." It is not a question of whether you have a strong or weak faith; but are you willing to live with the faith you have? For some persons, faith is a simple acceptance and uncluttered belief with few questions asked. Others find faith coming and going, strong at times and weak at other times because of the unpredictability of life's circumstances. For some it may be a wistful longing.

Since I am now living in post-retirement years, have I found answers to all my questions? The answer is no I have not, and frankly I am not sure I would be happy if I did.

I am helped by a quotation from the book, *Venture To The Innermost* by Van der Post. "Life is its own journey, presupposing its own change and movement, and one tries to arrest them at one's eternal peril."

I have found, as have thousands before me, that "to travel hopefully is a better thing than to arrive." God is asking us to be what we are and try to become what we are capable of becoming. In my journey of faith I have found some satisfying answers. I have found some part answers. I have found some nonanswers. I can live with that. True faith is to work and continue to gain enlightenment and strength. The Psalmist pointed out the way when he wrote..."*Be still, and know that I am God.*"

"And the things you have heard me say...will also be qualified to teach others."
—2 Timothy 2:2

Eve to Remember

William A. White

Her name was Eve Bacon and she was a dedicated and devoted Christian and member of the First Church of God in Jacksonville, Florida, located on the corner of Roosevelt Avenue and New Beach Boulevard, where Wilber Hatch was pastor. The year was 1954. Her husband then was a tall, humble man by the name of Herbert, whom she lovingly called Herbie. I became acquainted with Eve while I was in the Navy serving as an electrician and stationed in nearby Green Cove Springs, which was then the home of a mothball fleet of destroyers. She was a very gracious and friendly person, with a contagious desire to learn all she could about the Bible and the Church of God.

I can't quite recall all the exact particulars of our first meeting but it must have been in the church. I had gotten acquainted with a pretty girl by the name of Maxine King, who was also a member of that congregation. I remember that I couldn't go out with her unless I went to church with her, according to her mother. So, I did. Maxine was a member of a Sunday school class taught by Eve Bacon. It was then that I began a rich and most rewarding association with Sister Bacon. I don't believe I ever called her Eve. The Bible was central in her class and she took a real interest in the class members.

Not long after that, I began my journey with Jesus Christ as my Savior. I remember an evangelistic meeting at the church there with an evangelist named Margaret McCleskey. I remember going forward and kneeling at an altar and committing my life to Jesus Christ. Later Eve and her husband invited me to stay at their house on weekends so that I wouldn't have to drive back and forth from Green Cove Springs to Jacksonville. I remember well the in-depth conversations we used to have in her kitchen over coffee about her experience with the Lord and questions I had about the Bible.

Sister Bacon died in 1992, but her memory and influence live on in and through my life and I remain ever thankful to God for her concern and interest in me. I shall never forget the wonderful people of that church either.

Methodist Church
Cades Cove, Tennessee

"...If you seek him, he will be found by you..."
−1 Chronicles 28:9

Ground Zero Faith

Dondeena Bradley Ramey

aith is what you have to hold onto at the end of all the unanswered questions pounding in your head, and ultimately in your heart.

It was 8:45 A.M., Tuesday, September 11, 2001. It was one of those crisp autumn days in Manhattan and I was leisurely walking our daughter, Madison, to pre-school. We were excitedly talking through her routine and noticing how the morning sun was peeking through the trees. Allen, my husband, and I felt launched into a new phase of parenthood as we spent the previous evening attending orientation for new school-age parents. My cell phone rang–it was Allen. I did not answer it as I had my hands full with Madison's things and assumed I would call him after dropping her off in a few minutes. He immediately called back, so I answered, and as I listened I knew something was terribly wrong.

Faith is what you rely upon when the best day of your life suddenly can turn dark and full of uncertainty–waiting for answers.

Allen urgently asked if I had heard the news about the accidental airline crash into the tower at the World Trade Center. I had not. My immediate response was *get home* as we both knew how chaotic things would become downtown. He agreed. That unexpected dark day would then unfold, minute by minute, as the media would put together the surreal events of that horrible tragedy. I could not connect with Allen on our cell phones or home phone lines as telephone circuits were jammed and cell coverage was limited. I could only hope that he was headed home, while trying to let go of the grim fact that his office building, One Liberty, was directly across from the towers. The dreadful waiting began.

Faith is what you depend upon when you have to step outside that comfort zone into a melting pot of mixed belief systems.

I returned to the pre-school and brought Madison home as most parents did that day, but unfortunately, not all. Over 10,000 children

St. Paul's Chapel (1766) - *New York City, New York*

St. Paul's Chapel is located on Broadway between Vesey and Fulton Streets in New York City. It is the only pre-Revolutionary War building remaining in Manhattan. George Washington worshiped here regularly while he was President of the United States.

in the tri-state area lost one or two parents during this violent act. Tears flow at a moment's notice, there is rage, sadness, and feelings of helplessness in a time where so many have suffered loss. As I rocked Madison, waiting endless hours for some sign of Allen, I found myself prayerfully singing the hymns that I had learned as a child. *What a Mighty God We Serve, To God Be the Glory* and *Blessed Assurance* flooded back from my childhood memories. Reflecting on my own childhood, I longed for simpler times, being with family, spending summers with my grandparents. I can still see the little church upon the hill in Rich Creek where my parents were married. It was there I sang my first music solo surrounded by people who were interested in nurturing me. Little did I ever realize, until now, how much of an influence my own family's faith journey would be as a critical stepping stone for developing my own personal faith journey.

Faith is not abstract, but is a sacred, personal matter that requires a personal commitment.

Until recently, I am not sure I can honestly say that *faith* and how I nurtured it was something of which I was consciously aware. Growing up in a sports-minded family, the phrase "practice makes perfect" was readily accepted and carried out in many activities of my life. I suppose it is easier to follow the beliefs of family and friends than find one's own way. Now, however, the time came where those beliefs are personally challenged with a better understanding of my commitment to share and even defend my faith. I believe I am the last person to help anyone understand why that horrible act of terrorism occurred. But I am certain that God did not *allow* it to happen, as he gave each of us the right to choose him or to deny him. The Bible says *"seek and you will find Him"* and now I understand that I have to make the effort of faith to find Him.

Allen, covered with ash, was fortunate enough to make it home that afternoon after walking ten miles. Our daughter greeted him running, open arms, waiting for that big bear hug as on any other typical day. It was a priceless moment. It was also a turning point in our lives. For now we know more than ever that it is our personal faith, being witnessed by many, that will personally impact the lives of our own children.

"...he is my partner and fellow worker among you; as for our brothers, they are representatives of the churches and an honor to Christ."
—2 Corinthians 8:23

The Whole Nine Yards

Daniel C. Harman

Pastoring was our life. We'd been at it nearly twenty-five years, still had a thriving church, and yet had some unfulfilled goals. One was a dream about which we felt strongly. We longed to see a more vivid, more personal, more factual understanding between U. S. churches and the *mission field*. We wished that people could truly *see* the mission field. Then we met Chuck Thomas again, long after Anderson College days. From him we heard of Project Partner and its ministry of taking lay persons overseas, and we perked up.

To make a long story short, we found that to help him meant leaving the pastorate with no promise of any income, raising all funds needed to live, moving to Wichita from Louisville, and living by faith in a worldwide ministry, aimed mostly to third-world countries.

After wrestling a long time, I prayed, "God, if you're in this, make the way." He did.

Faith took on a new meaning as we moved at our expense, made a down payment on a house, and hauled two children, two cars and twenty-five years of stuff westward.

Betty Ann took care of stewardess duties on the ministry's airplane and acted as group hostess, while I traveled, spoke, and wrote, getting out the Project Partner word.

Our faith was rewarded.

Continued faith was required, desperately required.

We worked hard, never missed a payment on anything, traveled extensively, raised the children in a wholesome atmosphere, and kept house, cars, and dinner table in working order. Money came in without our ever asking for it, almost always from people we never dreamed would respond to what we were doing. We learned early on not to pinpoint people who *should give to help this ministry*. We

St. Paul Lutheran Church (1849) - *Milan, Indiana*

*St. Paul Lutheran Church in Milan, Indiana, was
founded on May 6, 1849. The congregation worships in
the oldest Lutheran Church building in the state.*

didn't ask for money, ever. No appeal whatsoever at any time, yet people seemed to sense the worth, the genuine quality of the ministry of the group.

And, oh, what rewards were heaped on us. People were touched, churches were revolutionized by missions, and people in many countries had a new lease on life because some *Americans* cared enough to come and lend a helping hand.

The move from Louisville was right.

Before this time and ever since then I have preached *faith*, mostly for salvation, for healing, for strength and wisdom to face each day's turmoil. And God has honored the word. But when it comes to money, I am a walking, talking, smiling, confident witness to God's ability to care for us, completely. If we trust God, He comes through for us. It's that simple to me.

There was this little church, in a house, where a sweet little lady lingered back after a service. We'd traveled a long way and told our story of reaching out to see what God was doing in other nations. The lady told us she wanted to help, and when we opened her letter weeks later it was one of the most impressive checks we ever got, a simple gesture of support that meant the world to the lady and lifted our faith another big notch; and, as God intended, helped some village beyond their wildest dreams or prayers.

When we trust, God takes over. Betty and I have learned to hang on to Him.

*"Ask and it will be given to you; seek and you will find;
knock and the door will be opened to you."*
—Matthew 7:7

Learning to Trust

James Earl Massey

I entered high school at Detroit's Cass Technical High School with great joy, but my leaving involved a bit of pain. On graduation night in June, 1947, I was rushing down the hall toward the room in which the music department graduates were to assemble. Mr. Glenn Klepinger, head of the music department, saw me and asked me to wait for a moment because he needed to discuss a problem that had come to his attention while examining my record of courses taken.

I waited with bated breath as Mr. Klepinger informed me about a course I had missed. "In screening your college entrance preparation subjects," he said, "I noticed that you had not taken English Composition Four, which all Cass graduates are required to take."

I listened, painfully anxious as he spoke, but an inner assurance soon steadied me and I replied that my advisor had allowed me to substitute a Speech course for the one in English Composition because of my plan to do pre-ministerial studies in college. Department chairman Klepinger looked intently at me, sensed my apparent dismay at being questioned about this at so late a time, then told me that he had discussed the matter with Principal William Stirton. The moment of pause before he gave the outcome of their discussion seemed like an eternity, but Mr. Klepinger went on to say that they had thought of letting me walk across the platform with my class, and that I could receive a dummy diploma to spare me embarrassment, and that I could return for a summer course in English Composition and thus complete the requirement. But after another brief pause, he went on to tell me what Principal Stirton had determined. The decision was that I would be graduated that night, as scheduled, and that the college to which I applied could determine how the apparent deficiency should be handled. Mr. Klepinger thought it a wise decision. So did I. Remembering that brief moment of pain, I walked across the platform of the auditorium that

Metropolitan Church of God (1954) - *Detroit, Michigan*

The history of the Church of God in Detroit would not be complete without mentioning the name of Daniel F. Oden. Born in Alabama, Oden served on the Missionary Board of the Church of God in 1909. The Church of God in Detroit grew from a small group of believers. When he heard of the need for pastoral leadership in Detroit, Rev. Oden, after much prayer, moved his family there.

James Earl Massey and followers from the Detroit Church began the Metropolitan Church of God in May, 1954. The congregation met in homes for a short while and then secured the use of the Danish Brotherhood Hall. The fellowship grew and in August, 1955, the facilities on Joy Street were acquired. The work continued to progress and the present building on Schaefer Highway was procured in July, 1971.

night very much aware that my life was in the hands of God. Clutching my diploma, I descended the stairs with mingled pride, praise, and humility.

The steadying "inner assurance" I had experienced was rooted in my understanding about the graciousness and guidance of God for all who look trustingly to Him; but it was also strengthened by successive experiences I had had of His assurance and help when faced with some problem or need. One such experience from that very period in my life well illustrates the basis for the assurance I felt as Mr. Klepinger and I talked that night before the graduation ceremony.

During that last year at Cass, with only a few weeks left before the expected June graduation, one afternoon I walked from school over to our church location on Detroit's West Side at Vermont and Hancock. As choir pianist, I wanted to practice my piano part before the choir rehearsal at church later that evening. After choir rehearsal, I stayed for the regular Friday night prayer vigil that most of the local ministers of the church attended. The prayer time ended rather late, so someone volunteered to drop me along the bus route that would get me home without having to change buses, as I always had to do if going out to where our family lived.

Once out of the car, standing at the bus stop under the streetlight, I suddenly realized that I had spent too much for lunch and did not have enough money left for my fare home. I felt in my pocket and located only four pennies, but a full fare was ten cents! I began praying.

I was praying that God would let someone drive by who might recognize me and offer a ride. Several cars whizzed by, but no one stopped. I continued praying, and soon remembered the spare nickel I kept stashed away in a secret pocket of my wallet. I opened the wallet and extracted the nickel, grateful for the memory. But I still had only nine cents when I needed ten. It occured to me that I could get on the bus and risk asking the driver to let me ride with paying less than the full fare, but I felt too embarrassed and dismissed the thought.

As I continued praying, aloud, I began walking. In the course of finishing a block I was aware that my foot had kicked a coin. I stopped suddenly, listened intently to the sound of the rolling coin, and went over to where I thought it had stopped. Reaching down I felt around on the sidewalk, located the coin, and rushed to the nearest streetlight to see what I had found. It was a penny! My heart was pounding anxiously as I reached into my pocket to see if perchance I had dropped *(and found)* one of the four pennies I knew I had. The four other pennies were still there. When the bus came, I entered, sat down, and continued giving God thanks for answering my prayer. I had needed ten cents to pay my fare, and God had provided the needed penny to complete that amount! That was but one of the many experiences which deepened my sense of assurance about the mindfulness of God toward my life and its needs.

James Earl Massey

While growing up at home we were constantly reminded that God is the source of all that blesses our life. We began every meal with thanksgiving to God for the good gift of food, and we closed every day with thanksgiving for all the other needs which had been met. Life and teaching at church steadily deepened what we heard read and said at home. There were many readings we heard from scripture about God as provider, and we were even encouraged to memorize them. I cannot begin to number the times I heard my father or mother speak so appreciatively about the goodness and mercies of the Lord. They spoke out of our family's experience of accented needs during the awesome Depression years. Even now, many years afterward, the memory of how God provided for us during those years remains fresh in my mind. As Roger Hazelton, one of my teachers at Oberlin Seminary used to say to us, "Prayer is nothing without the living trust that what we need, God has to give us."

Jesus encouraged us with this promise: *"Ask and it will be given you; seek and you will find; knock and the door will be opened to you."* *–Matthew 7:7* That instruction taught me the importance of prayer for my needs, and it stirs me so to pray. We ask; God grants. I have stated the matter simply here, although it has taken a lifetime of experience to clear away some misunderstandings that blocked my faith and dulled my focus as I sought to correlate my anxious askings with God's multiple and ready provisions.

*"For it is by grace you have been saved, through faith—
and this not from yourselves, it is the gift of God."*
—*Ephesians 2:8*

Saved by Faith

Richard H. Petersen

The picture is of the Village United Methodist Church in Waldoboro, Maine. Waldoboro, on Maine's mid-coast, was famous during the nineteenth century for the five-masted schooners built there. I served this and two other churches on the Waldoboro Circuit, but my conversion to Jesus Christ took place a decade earlier.

I was a field engineer for an industrial electrical motor manufacturer, with western Massachusetts as my sales territory. My wife, two little boys, and I moved from our native Connecticut to the city of Northampton, Massachusetts. When we drove into town to take up our new residence, I remember seeing the sign "The Rev. Jonathan Edwards Preached Here." Soon I had a house, a mortgage, a new car, a dynamic job, and another son on the way, as Zorba the Greek said: "The full catastrophe." Then we got active in the Methodist Church, and I heard the gospel of salvation by grace through faith alone in Jesus Christ, who died on the cross for our sins and rose for our justification. Wow! What a simple message. I've always thought that the Holy Spirit was still running around in the city where the Great Awakening of the eighteenth century began, and He sought me and found me.

I quit my job, entered Duke Divinity School, served Methodist churches in Cedar Grove, North Carolina, added a daughter to our family, earned a Ph.D. at Duke, and then went up to Waldoboro to continue to preach the gospel. By the time I got to Portland, Maine, I met David and Avis Liverett and their son Mark.

It's all so simple, isn't it? God loves you. Salvation is a gift. He gives you forgiveness and self-esteem. I am a child of God. I can do all things through Christ. I will love Him and my neighbor as myself and it's life's greatest challenge, to be conformed to the image of His Son.

Village United Methodist Church
Waldoboro, Maine

My favorite verses: *"For it is by grace you have been saved, through faith—and this not from yourselves, it is the gift of God—not by works, so that no one can boast. For we are God's workmanship, created in Christ Jesus to do good works, which God prepared in advance for us to do." —Ephesians 2:8-10*

It's all there: grace, faith, gift, humility, new creation, a life of good works wrought in God.

I served the Methodist Church for almost twenty years, went on to continue my ministry in the Evangelical Covenant Church, and in my retirement I still preach the simple message: God loves us, He gives us forgiveness and new life, and the greatest thing we can do is love Him and one another. It all

Richard H. Petersen

started for me nearly fifty years ago in a small city in Massachusetts. What a wonderful life!

*"And the God of all grace, who called you to his eternal glory in Christ,
after you have suffered a little while, will himself restore you
and make you strong, firm and steadfast."*
—1 Peter 5:10

A Private Decision

Amy Dudeck Witt

The white frame building with four windows on each side, a country church with a belfry over the door, had nothing yet everything to do with my faith journey.

As a young child, sitting on a bench pew, I dutifully heard long sermon-lectures about the ferocious scary pictures on the chart stretched across the front of the church. I did grasp that these pictures told about the Bible book of Revelation. During the remainder of those nights I was traumatized with nightmares. My well-meaning parents never knew of my dilemma. However, I have ever after avoided reading in the book of Revelation.

Long before this time, my paternal grandmother, of Swiss Lutheran background, had attended a community meeting by a traveling evangelistic team. This particular group was led by a D. S. Warner representing a reformation called Church of God. She, with several isolated neighbors, became dedicated, steadfast believers.

Years later, my grandmother, living with us, became the dominant pervasive personality in our home climate. The over-riding code was no mingling with non-believers. For me this meant no school friends. In retrospect and for later information, our family, though well established, were the outcasts in the community.

My mother, by my grandmother, was considered a non-believer, much of the time. Her church background was Swiss Evangelical Reform. Having to remove her wedding band, my mother told me later she saw no wrong in wearing it. She saw no connection with the ring and her faith in her Heavenly Father.

Despite the daily admonishments, during my teen years, I regarded the Bible stories my mother had read to us important. And though I prayed, being thankful for nature and things about me, there was a subtle desire and need.

Through music, my personal journey of faith really began.

Fellowship Baptist Church (1840)
Hamilton County, Indiana

Practicing the hymns for my piano lesson one day I sensed a real need to stop and pray, asking God to be the guide of my life. Thus, very quietly, came the beginning of my private walk of faith.

Faith for life's journey with God cannot be attached to a person—family member, friend, leader—I learned and continue learning. The frailties and foibles of human nature and personalities are an inevitable fact. The walk of faith goes through the ups and downs of personal living that present constant efforts and challenges.

Generation to Generation
Celebrating the Teaching Church

By Christie Smith Stephens

Generation to Generation, Jesus Loves Us, This We Know;
Generation to Generation, The Love of God Unfolds.

Through centuries of learning, the Light of Truth is passed,
Etched in stone tablets, Incarnate Teaching Word.
The Ever-New Old Story, Wisdom's Legacy,
The Birthright, most precious, Of God's Family.
To those who've walked before us, our grateful hearts we give;
For those who follow our steps, Faithfully we'll live;
As Children of God, Every race and creed,
We reach across divisions in Peace for Unity.

Generation to Generation, Jesus Loves Us, This We Know;
Generation to Generation, The Love of God Unfolds.

God adds to the Church those being saved
By knowledge of The Word, Lived lessons of faith;
Sisters and Brothers, Families Diverse,
We sing Love's song together throughout the universe.
We celebrate The Church, A Teaching Ministry.
We celebrate The Word, The Truth that sets us free.
We celebrate All People, God's Family.
We celebrate The Hope Who Lives Eternally.

Generation to Generation, Jesus Loves Us, This We Know.
Generation to Generation, The Love of God Unfolds.
Age to Age, we tell The Story.
Age to Age, we sing The Song.
Generation to Generation, The Teaching Church of God Moves On...
Generation to Generation, The Teaching Church Moves On...
Amen.

"Now faith is being sure of what we hope for and certain of what we do not see."
—Hebrews 11:1

A Simple Path to Faith

Kenneth F. Hall

I thank God for the songs we sing and hear that lead us on the pathway of faith. How impoverished we would be without them.

I thank God for the sermons we hear week after week helping us understand what faith is all about. How to apply it to the tests of life. How to practice it. And how to put it into practical, everyday service.

I thank God for the great churches where I have worshiped, soaring cathedrals and small neighborhood chapels. High vaulted arches, inspiring stained-glass windows lift my soul to God and to greater faith in Him.

But I especially thank God for an entirely different expression of faith that I experienced in my youngest years. The scene would be a simple old Quaker meeting house built just after the Civil War. Its straight-backed benches were long ago put together by folks in the meeting and provided one narrow board to sit on and two slats to lean back against, if you were older and bigger than I was at age four. The wooden floor was there to magnify and re-echo every stirring sound you would make. Down front would be benches where the elders of the meeting would sit facing the rest of us. No musical instruments. No altars. Plain glass windows. All the wood painted gray.

It was here that I as a four-year-old would sit between my parents for a long, long hour, squirming on the bench, mind wandering afar—to God, now and then, and off to my toys at home. Maybe I would play with my shoe, and off it would finally slip, only to drop like a thunderbolt in the silence of the meeting onto the wooden floor below. But it was also here where my eyes would wander down to the facing benches where I would see my aging grandparents sitting in their plain Quaker garments. And now and then, Grandfather would read a passage from the Bible. Once in a

Sandwich Meeting of Friends (1657) - *Sandwich, Massachusetts*

Sandwich Monthly Meeting of Friends was established in 1657 and is the oldest continuous Quaker meeting in North America. It consists of congregations in Sandwich, West Falmouth and Yarmouth. This meeting house is the third on this site and was built in 1810.

long while my grandmother would pray aloud in this mostly silent meeting. Occasionally another elder would give a brief testimony.

In this simple, uncluttered setting I could see the honest, open faces of my grandparents. Amidst all the discomforts and difficulties of being a four-year-old in a silent meeting I could feel the devotion of my parents. Somewhere there in those moments I started to have a glimpse of what true faith means as it reflects itself in the trust of a four-year-old for the God upheld by these plain people.

In such a setting I started to learn at least the beginnings of what Hebrews 11:1-2 teaches: *"Faith is the assurance of things hoped for, the conviction of things not seen. Indeed by faith our ancestors received approval."*

Kenneth F. Hall

"I have been reminded of your sincere faith, which first lived in your grandmother Lois and in your mother Eunice and, I am persuaded, now lives in you also."
−2 Timothy 1:5

Hand Me Down Faith

Arlo F. Newell

Being the youngest of three boys in the Newell family, hand-me-downs were a part of growing up. Whether it was a pair of OshKosh B'Gosh bib overalls or a Schwinn bicycle that was once new, each had previously been worn by or owned by Marion or Don before it got to Arlo. Did I value them less because the fabric had faded or the paint on the bicycle had been chipped? Have I carried some psychological trauma into adult life because I was not given something new? No, not really! To be truthful, I was proud of my brothers, they were my heroes, my examples. Most of the time I wanted to be like them, even to the point of trying to act like them. When receiving a hand-me-down I took pride in the fact that now that particular possession belonged to me, I claimed it as my own.

While some hand-me-downs are soon worn out, discarded and forgotten, there are others that should be treasured because of sentimental value and historical significance to the family. They become heirlooms which are more valuable the longer they are passed on to the next generation. Hand-me-downs may become a part of our legacy, our inheritance.

Paul uses the term as he writes regarding the faith of his son in the ministry, Timothy, *"...what a rich faith it is, HANDED DOWN from your grandmother Lois to your mother Eunice, and now to you."*
−2 Timothy 1:5

This was no genetic transmission like DNA, or a type of Christian clone. The reference is to the Christian faith, values which characterized Timothy's family for at least three generations. While saving grace is not transmitted genetically, there is a sense in which the characteristics of spiritual sensitivity and moral behavior are passed on from generation to generation. The very atmosphere of the family is conducive to developing a personal belief system in which Jesus Christ is Lord. The ancient Jewish confession in

St. James Catholic Church (1852) - *Thomaston, Maine*

At first the Catholic community in the Thomaston area lacked numbers and had no settled place of worship. In 1852, the poor farm on Meadow Road was purchased and services were held in the house on the farm. The gift of the Congregational meeting house supplied the needs for the next forty years as it was a beautiful edifice and in a good location. In 1915, the old church had become almost impossible to heat. It was decided to tear down the grand old building in favor of a more comfortable and up-to-date structure. On October, 24, 1915, the first High Mass was celebrated in the new building.

Deuteronomy 6:4-9, prepared one for the understanding and acceptance of the faith handed down by the family.

Exposed to authentic Christian faith lived out by both grandmother and mother, Timothy claimed this hand-me-down faith as his own. Two times in the verse Paul refers to the genuineness and certitude of Timothy's faith. What was handed down? An example of the Christian faith, which he claimed as his own.

Many times in our family it was necessary for me to grow into the hand-me-downs passed on to me by my brothers. The overalls were not the right size or the bicycle was too tall, requiring that I mature before being able to make full use of them. Hand-me-down faith is like that, many times requiring that I stretch, develop, mature before being able to appropriate the faith passed on to me. My faith in God, my understanding of the Bible, and my relationships in the church, continue to require personal spiritual growth.

At my retirement dinner given by Warner Press in 1993, a Kodak moment came for me when my friend, Marc Clarke, sang the song, *"May those who come behind us find us faithful."* As Marc sang, I took note of those present—my wife, our children, my colleagues in the editorial department and a host of friends. I thought also of people I had pastored, young preachers with whom I worked, and the communities in which we had lived. Then I asked myself the question, "Have I been faithful in handing on to them the faith in Christ which others gave to me?"

The task of the church is intergenerational, from generation to generation. We have all been shaped and molded by hand-me-downs from those who came before us. Nobody gets here without a grandmother, Timothy didn't, nor did we. The future of the church is dependent upon the transmission of faith to those who come behind us. Faith handed down to me by my parents, pastors, teachers and friends convinced me that I wanted this Christian faith for my very own.

Of course I had to stretch and grow to believe that *"all things are possible to them that believe"* but I claimed it as my own and now I hand it on to those who come after me. Without hand-me-downs we lose touch with our roots, no longer connected with our inheritance from the past. Here is a hand-me-down faith that may be a bit faded from the years and it may require that you stretch to believe, but it is true that *"the victory that overcomes the world...is our faith."* –1 John 5:4.

"Therefore put on the full armor of God, so that when the day of evil comes, you may be able to stand your ground, and after you have done everything, to stand."
—Ephesians 6:13

Standing Ground

Kathleen Davey Buehler

At times along my journey of faith I am called upon not to go but to stand. For me that's a tall order. Standing is not something I do very well. Walking? Certainly. Pacing? Yes. Running? On occasion. Storming around? Often. But not standing.

To me standing is not doing. And that's what I want. I want to do, to fix things.

Remember Gideon's army of three hundred? They had a torch in a jar in one hand and a trumpet in the other hand, and they were told to stand and wait for the signal. Had I been there, I probably would have jumped before the signal, breaking the jar and racing down the hill like a crazy person.

Recently I've been called upon to stand, to wait, to see what God is going to do in some situations I so desperately want to fix and with persons I so anxiously want to help. I've had to stand by and see these persons I love in deep pain and realize that there is nothing I can do to lessen that hurt. I've had to remind myself once again that I am not the healer, not the helper, not the savior. God is. God loves these persons and me and is working out good plans in our lives.

Standing ground and waiting to see what God will do is a hard lesson to learn, especially for a *doer* like me. But it's part of the journey, and I'm committed to staying on this journey until I reach the end.

So I'll hold the light of faith closely, keep the victory trumpet near at hand, and endeavor to stand.

East Side Church of God (1951) - *Anderson, Indiana*

In 1949 and 1950 people from Park Place Church of God and South Meridian Church of God agreed to plant a church to meet the needs of the young families moving into the east side of Anderson. On September 17, 1950, the congregation assembled to break ground for East Side Church of God. Classrooms and the minister's study were on the first floor. The sanctuary and nursery were located on the second floor. The first service was held on August 5, 1951, and Reverend Floyd Tunnell became the congregation's first full-time pastor.

There have been three more sanctuaries built since 1951 to accommodate the expansion of size in the congregation. The current sanctuary was constructed in 1986 and has an average attendance of approximately 1,400 people on Sunday morning in two services. Approximately 4,000 people call East Side Church of God their church home.

"Look at the birds of the air; they do not sow or reap or store away in barns, and yet your heavenly Father feeds them. Are you not of more value than they? Who of you by worrying can add a single hour to his life?"
—Matthew 6:26-27

Getting on Airplanes as an Act of Faith

Merle D. Strege

In nearly all respects my life has been insulated from tragedy, harm, and even insecurity. I was raised in a home where I knew that my father and mother loved my sister, my brothers, and me. My family members–my wife, our sons and their wives, and now our little granddaughter–are healthy and whole physically and spiritually. For twenty-five years I have worked at a calling that I could never refer to merely as a job. The world I have experienced for more than a half century I have known to be safe, orderly, and where I was largely in control of the situation. I have followed Jesus for more than forty years, but trusting God was not difficult in such a world. The events of September 11, 2001, dramatically altered my sense of peace and order.

Since the World Trade Center attack, all Americans have been made to realize that our lives are not nearly as secure as we previously believed. *"In a New York minute,"* as the Eagles sing, *"everything can change."* In the blink of an eye something as mundane as boarding an airplane took on ultimate significance. Like many Americans I began to fear flying, and when my wife and I were booked on a flight less than a month following the terrorist attacks, I chose to drive instead. My comfortable, secure life had not prepared me to trust God as fully as Jesus teaches his followers; unprepared, I was afraid.

Another month passed before I was to make another flight. I spent much of that time considering the idea that faith is, as Paul Tillich defined it, "ultimate concern;" simply, faith is to trust in that which concerns us ultimately. It occurred to me that since I was prepared to trust God with my death I also ought to trust God with my life. No longer able to secure my existence–as if I ever was,

First Church of God (1952) - *Minneapolis, Minnesota*

The message of the Church of God first came to the Minneapolis area to a group of Hungarian-speaking people. Andrew Kandler, who had come from Canada in 1906, was one of them. He had heard of the Church of God from a church in Winnipeg, started by Karl Arbeiter. This group originally met in Como Park (St. Paul). The St. Paul Church reached out to assist a group in Minneapolis by helping them buy a lot at 38th Street and 38th Avenue for a future church building. In 1946, Marvin Forbes came to be the pastor in St. Paul. Four and a half years later he began a work in Minneapolis and moved there.

The church in Minneapolis first met in homes. One of these homes was that of Charles M. Schulz, the cartoonist of "Peanuts" fame. Schulz became acquainted with the Church of God when his mother was ill with cancer. He was present when the pastor of the St. Paul Church visited her and served communion. He later testified of that service, "It was one of the richest memories I have." He was won to evangelical Christianity and the Church of God through this ministry.

I looked to God to secure it instead. Armed with that insight, a few days later I boarded my flight with C. W. Naylor's words playing through my head: *Whether upon the land, or on the stormy deep; When 'tis serene and calm, or when the wild winds blow, I shall not be afraid–I am the Lord's, I know.*

I Am the Lord's, I Know

Charles W. Naylor, 1874-1950   D. Otis Teasley, 1876-1942

*"The grace of our Lord was poured out on me abundantly,
along with the faith and love that are in Christ Jesus."*
—1 Timothy 1:14

Two Hands of Faith

Hollis S. Pistole

Last summer I attended a Pistole family reunion near Sparta, Tennessee, where I was born. Following the meeting, several of us went to the Pistole Baptist Church that my forefathers helped to start in 1851. It still has an active congregation today. Nearby was the Pistole cemetery where several family members are buried. Among them was my great grandfather, Stephen Pistole, deacon and clerk at the church. Later my grandfather James was also the church clerk. Standing there in that tranquil setting of the rolling hills of middle Tennessee, I reminisced with thoughts of my family heritage and my faith, which was nurtured there.

I remembered attending a revival service when I was five years old and was so stirred by the powerful sermon that I began to cry. My parents consoled me, but felt I was too young to make a commitment of faith. From childhood I had positive feelings about faith and love for God.

One of my most meaningful lessons of faith came shortly after that while walking with my own father. As a police officer he made an impressive appearance of six foot three, solidly built on a 230 pound frame, dressed in a khaki uniform with a Stetson hat, badge, gun in a holster strapped to his gun belt, with handcuffs and keys dangling on a chain. His work was primarily at the courthouse and he often walked home.

Between his station and our house was an old cemetery. Kids found it a place to play among the tombstones and tell *ghost* stories. But at night it was a *spooky* place where we suspected the ghosts came out. On occasion my older brother and I would go to walk home with Dad after work. But this time my brother was unable to go and I went alone. It was in the fall and the days were getting shorter and shadows were gathering as I hurried past the

Pistole Baptist Church (1851) - *Sparta, Tennessee*

Situated near Sparta, amid the rolling hills of middle Tennessee, this church was constituted as a Baptist mission in 1851. Built of native lumber with subsequent additions over the years, the church still serves a flourishing congregation. A short distance away is the Pistole Cemetery. In the western migration from Virginia in the early 1800s, a few Pistole families settled in this area and shared in the church's beginning.

The congregation thrived until the outbreak of the Civil War. Divided loyalties and guerrilla warfare wrought havoc, disrupted the community and resulted in the disbanding of the congregation. After the war ended a nucleus of former members began meeting and refurbishing the church. By 1874, the church had become a healing force in the community and was duly recognized by the Baptist Association. That faithful ministry continues to this day.

cemetery. I met my father and we started home along with the jingle of his keys, handcuffs and the creaking leather of his gun holster. I reached for his hand and felt his reassuring clasp. Now I had no fear of the *spooks*. In my imagination, I even wished that some of the *ghosts* might leap out at me. Then they would see what a powerful force my father was—he would smash and utterly demolish them!

That evening when I said my *good night prayers* and relived the happy walk with my father, my thoughts also turned to those about my Heavenly Father. I didn't grasp the true meaning of God's love and mercy at that time, yet I was comforted by the awareness of a *divine being*. In the years that followed I have claimed the memory of that experience time and again. By faith I have reached out my anxious hand to my Lord for His added strength.

Hollis S. Pistole

Now with joy I can say that He has not failed to sustain me through many troublesome times. And today I continue to reach for my Heavenly Father's unchanging hand and know that He will guide me safely home, even as I did as a child when I walked hand in hand with my own father. A life touched by two *hands*—one human, one divine. Trust in the human father nurtured the child; faith in the divine Father leads to abundant life now and for eternity.

"But because of his great love for us, God, who is rich in mercy, made us alive with Christ even when we were dead in transgressions—it is by grace you have been saved."
—Ephesians 2:4

The Altar

Richard L. Willowby

My mother described me as her altar boy. She did not mean an acolyte. I usually went to the altar by by the third verse of the invitation hymn. Oscar Borden, pastor of the Redline Church of God in Palco, Kansas, once told me I couldn't come back for two weeks. I was scared to death; what if I died that week. It was two very careful weeks.

My tender conscience and a faulty theology of Christian perfection brought me to the altar at the close of nearly every service. I practiced a negative interpretation of Charles Sheldon's question from his classic book, *In His Steps,* "What would Jesus do?"

Over the years, however, I have learned something about grace. Still, I am thankful for that old altar and the God who met me there and walks with me everyday. Now I kneel at the altar of the church I pastor and pray for those who will hear me preach. I pray for forgiveness when I need it, for strength and for guidance.

When I was managing editor of *Vital Christianity,* I saw Wilda Anderson, my primary Sunday school teacher. "Richard, you're such an encouragement to me," she said. "Oh, Sister Anderson," I replied (feeling a little too full of myself) "How is that?" She answered, "I never thought anyone who went to the altar as often as you would ever make it." I haven't made it yet, but I am on the journey.

I have pieces of wood that made up the altar at the Redline Church. After the beautiful new facility was completed, my dad rescued them from the old building for me. I remember my mother telling me how my grandfather lovingly shaped the altar with hand tools in the light of a kerosene lamp.

I want to make something symbolic from that wood made sacred by my grandfather's skilled, loving hands and the tears that fell on it across the years. Suggestions are welcome.

Anderson Campmeeting Tabernacle (1918) - *Anderson, Indiana*

The "wooden tabernacle" with a sawdust floor was built in 1918 at a cost of $25,000. It was planned as the largest auditorium of its kind in the world, rivaling the size of the Mormon Tabernacle in Salt Lake City, Utah. Although it fell short of the expectations, it did grow to seat 8,000 people.

The establishment of the General Ministerial Assembly in 1917 created the need for a central campmeeting. Gifted speakers and musicians were always featured during this mid-June gathering. World Service Day began in 1940 and the use of a giant thermometer recorded the giving during the gathering.

"...God's abundant provision of grace and of the gift of righteousness reign in life through the one man, Jesus Christ."
—Romans 5:17

Extended Grace

Forrest R. Robinson

"I was so foolish and undisciplined," I told myself as I drove feverishly to the hospital. I had allowed myself to put off leaving far too long and now I was afraid I would miss seeing this dear old sister before her surgery, which everyone felt could be life threatening.

My tires squealed as I came into the hospital parking lot. I jumped out of my car and tried not to look conspicuous as I walked to the front door. One good thing, I did not have to stop for directions. Everyone knew me and I also knew them, in this small town where my ministry was putting down roots.

As I turned the corner to the surgery waiting room, my heart leaped into my throat. She was not there—I had missed her! "This saint deserved a better pastor than I," I told myself, when suddenly I realized the nurse was telling me that my friend was still in the hall and I could still pray for her.

Redeemed, I quickly got to my dear little friend who broke into a great big smile. As I took her hand my panic now froze me. All those wonderful words of assurance I wanted to comfort her with stopped in my throat! After a moment, my little lady patted my hand and said, "Don't you worry, Pastor, everything will be all right." And it was. It was all right because God was with my friend through the surgery. It was all right because God taught me a very valuable lesson. He is not dependent on us doing everything right for Him to work. He was well aware of the love and concern I had for my friend. He was well aware of my friend's need. We need always to remember that He is present when we need Him.

Wherever you are in life, do the very best you can but never make the mistake that God's best comes only when we do our best. His grace extends to cover our mistakes.

Shady Grove Church of God (1938) - *Paducah, Kentucky*

Two revivals in 1938, resulted in the organization of Shady Grove Church of God. The congregation first met in the Shady Grove School. Land was purchased on January 20, 1940, and timber was donated. The frame was erected but finances were limited. Some of the men were called to military service and the project was halted for two years. In 1942, the building was completed with Forrest Robinson's grandfather serving on the Board of Trustees.

*"Therefore, since we have been justified through faith, we have peace
with God through our Lord Jesus Christ, through whom we have
gained access by faith into this grace in which we now stand...."*
—Romans 5:1-2

Church by the Side of the Road

Kenneth E. Crouch

This "church by the side of the road" burned to the
ground in 1953. Within two years Eden United Church
of Christ rebuilt, bigger and better. The rural congregation
near Muncie, Indiana, pulled together to pay off the resulting
debt and build a parsonage during the next ten years.

Tragedy can overcome a people, or challenge them to move
forward with courage and faith. This congregation chose the latter
path and continues to be a vital community of faith.

This is not surprising when one discovers that most of its
members have come from farming families. Each year these ministers
of the soil begin preparing the land and planting the seed that they
hope will bring a livable yield. They operate on faith as they hope
for enough rain at the right times, as they pray for no late frosts in
the spring or early frosts in the fall.

In 1953, many of the members had married in the spring or
summer of 1929. Married life began with "for richer or poorer."
Little did they know that they would be severely tested in the
months and years after the great depression hit in October of that
year. But they persevered and were among those who survived.

In the decade following the fire, three men answered the call to
ordained ministry. Three of their sons followed them. Is it not
amazing how faith begets faith!

Eden Congregational Christian Church (1905) - *Muncie, Indiana*

Eden church was also known as "The Church by the Side of the Road." The construction of a cement walk from the church to the old electric railway station one half mile east called McCormick Stop helped in giving the church this name. In 1929, the General Convention of Christian Churches merged with the National Council of Congregational Churches. At that time the church became Eden Congregational Christian Church.

On October 5, 1953, disaster struck and the church was burned to the ground. In 1955, a new building was dedicated. In May, 1962, the Congregational Christian Churches merged with the Evangelical and Reformed Churches. The Eden Church became the Eden United Church of Christ.

"I will sing to the LORD all my life; I will sing praise to my God as long as I live."
—*Psalm 104:33*

⚬⚬⚬

Mile-Markers
of Faith

Joy L. May

*N*o place is so dear to my childhood as the little brown church in the vale. If I close my eyes, I can still hear my father's voice ringing in the car singing the basso pedal tones of that old hymn tune *Come, come, come, come*. Mom's breathy soprano singing the melody and my young untrained ear picking out alto and tenor alternately, finding whatever notes mom and dad weren't singing. These are the memories I have of childhood years winding through the Smoky Mountains on the Cades Cove loop, looking at tiny, weather-beaten buildings, each of them a home to the Father, though with different denominational names adorning the doors. And our annual trips to Bee Spring in southern Tennessee, where the tiny white church was so bright with light from the cracks in between the planks in the walls and so cold with drafts from the holes in the floor.

My family has always traveled together, weaving around on the back-roads of Ohio and Tennessee. And we've always sung together, too. Hymns were the natural choice in the car. Since Dad was a music minister, we all knew the words to just about every hymn of the church. And every song had at least four verses. That would get you a good few miles down the road. We picked the songs that seemed to correspond with the weather and the environment; *It Is Well* always seemed to be the song we'd sing when it started raining (though we sometimes changed the chorus from *It is well with my soul* to be *It is wet on the road!*) and *Sunshine in My Soul* worked well for really warm, sunny days. I suppose that's how we happened on *Little Brown Church in the Vale* as our favorite when we spotted old country churches.

Granted, Mom and Dad knew the tune and the lyrics much better than I. But I caught on after hearing it enough. And the words of that refrain were so true for me. In fact, lyrics of many hymns were the

The Little Brown Church in the Vale (1864) - *Nashua, Iowa*

William Pitts, a young music teacher, wrote a song called "Church in the Wildwood" based on his vision of a church in the midst of some ancient trees that he had seen while on a trip in Bradford, Iowa. Upon his return, he discovered a small church had been built in the very spot he had visualized in his hymn. This song brought thousands of couples of all denominations to be married in its peaceful, charming, rustic atmosphere. The official name of the church is the Congregational Eclessiastical Society of Old Bradford Iowa. For all public use it is called "The Little Brown Church." Construction on the church began in 1860 and by the end of 1862 the building was enclosed. All material and labor had been donated. When it came to painting the building, the cheapest paint to be found was Ohio Mineral Paint in an unhappy brown shade. William Pitts had written a song for a church that wasn't there. The congregation had painted the church without ever hearing of the song.

mile-markers of my faith journey during those drives with my parents. I never realized how sweetly they spoke of my life then or now.

My parents own cassettes of my voice at age two and age five. Recorded on old, warped audiotapes is my tiny voice, thick with the slow drawl of the South, belting out, *I am a child of God, I am a child of God. I have 'warshed' my robes in th' cleanin' fountain. I am a child of God.* From the earliest years of my life, though I may not have understood the depth of the words nor known them all correctly I knew who I was: God's child.

As I grew, and learned to sing harmony with my family, we often sang *Consecration* because the alto line was pretty straightforward and easy to sing. But its theology and testimony are what I find eases my spirit today: *I care not where my Lord directs, His purpose I'll fulfill. I know He everyone protects who does His holy will.* As an adult, the Lord has directed me to places I never thought I'd go, and often didn't want to, but I can hear that tight harmony above the drone of road noise and I'm lulled into a peaceful acceptance of *Where He leads me I will follow.*

Still, of all the songs that fill my mind, none brings a smile to me as much as *The Church in the Wildwood.* And it isn't because all the lyrics speak to all my life experiences. It's more that I hold on to that *place...so dear to my childhood.* That place wasn't the churches, houses of worship where I was accustomed to meeting Jesus, but it was the backseat of every car we've ever owned, where I learned to sing the anthems that make the church what it is.

The buildings are sacred, but the gospel preached from their pulpits and sung from their pews by the people of God, the body of Christ, His bride, the Church are just as precious. Precious enough to be transported to the inside of a family vehicle where, passing them one by one, we honored those places and the message they contained by singing their song: *How sweet on a clear Sabbath morning, to list to the clear ringing bell; its tones so sweetly are calling, Oh, come to the church in the vale.*

The Little Brown Church in the Vale

The Church in the Wildwood

William S. Pitts   William S. Pitts

1. There's a church in the val-ley by the wild-wood, No love-li-er
2. How sweet on a clear, Sab-bath morn-ing, To list to the
3. There, close by the church in the val-ley, Lies one that I
4. There, close by the side of that loved one, 'Neath the tree where the

place in the dale; No spot is so dear to my child-hood As the
clear ring-ing bell; Its tones so sweet-ly are call-ing, Oh,
loved so well; She sleeps, sweetly sleeps 'neath the wil-low, Dis-
wild flow-ers bloom, When the fare-well hymn shall be chant-ed, I shall

D. S.—*spot is so dear to my child-hood As the*

FINE. CHORUS.

lit-tle brown church in the vale.
come to the church in the vale.
turb not her rest in the vale.
rest by her side in the tomb.   Oh, come, come, come, come, come, come,

Come to the

lit-tle brown church in the vale.

D.S.

church in the wild-wood, Oh, come to the church in the dale;   No
come, come, come, come, come, come, come, come, come, come, come, come, come,

"My feet stand on level ground; in the great assembly I will praise the LORD."
—Psalm 26:12

Level Ground Spirituality

W. Malcolm Rigel

everal stories have circulated of an incident which happened many years ago at Calvary Baptist Church in Washington, D. C. One account was like this: among the persons who had come forward to become members of the church were a Chinese immigrant, Ah Sing, a woman who cleaned houses for a living, and the Honorable Charles Evans Hughes, a justice of the U. S. Supreme Court. Noting the variety of persons before him, the pastor said, "My friends, at the cross of Christ the ground is level."

In a recent early morning quiet time I was reading Psalm 26 when verse twelve especially got my attention: *"My feet stand on level ground; in the great assembly I will praise the LORD."* Immediately the story of Ah Sing, the cleaning woman, Judge Hughes, the pastor's statement and this Psalm's basic truth were linked together. I was awakened to a challenge of Christian living and witness not totally embraced before.

I began to recall several rural or small town churches I had served over the years. Most of them were in humble buildings made of concrete blocks or framed with wood siding. The people who came to worship were humble farmers, factory workers, miners, merchants, teachers, students and homemakers. At the cross of Christ we're all on level ground. But did we practice that?

As I now think of it, I must confess I did not always act as if we were on the same level. I let education, denomination, manner of dress, speech, possessions, skin color or geographic background create a tragic caste system. Even more tragic, some of us holiness and conservative church people acted as the Pharisees of Jesus' day! We thought we had a more reasoned biblical theology or at least a more mystical and emotional expression of Christian faith. However,

New Salem First Church of God (1894) - Salem, Indiana

During the winter of 1894, two ministers, J. P. Keeling and Jeremiah Cole came into the New Salem area. They preached a message that attracted many people. In 1918, the New Salem church building was purchased by the Church of God. The building had been built by the Christian Church in 1888 and 1889 and was moved to the present location in 1921.

neither of these nor any other reason was cause for us to see ourselves on a higher plain of spirituality. We had failed to recognize that God alone measures spirituality.

I used to think I knew enough scripture to present an irrefutable positional argument for the Holy Spirit according to a certain holiness-pietistic stance. One Sunday morning I thought I made a *perfect* presentation of this Bible truth. I had preached a brilliant sermon! However, afterward, as I was greeting my congregation at the door, a recent convert gave me a shocking judgment. "Your sermon was all true so far as you know." I suddenly realized that at best, *"...I know in part;..."* *–1 Corinthians 13:12b.* Such a humbling God-sent spiritual correction made forty years ago has never left me. It showed me what level ground spirituality is all about, and that same lesson is with me yet today. After this experience I could begin to follow through with the rest of the verse from Psalms, *"in the great assembly (congregation) I will praise the Lord."*

Malcolm Rigel

My prayer is, "Lord, keep reminding me that the Christ came down to my level so that I might live on level ground with all peoples, Amen."

"I thank my God every time I remember you.
In all my prayers for all of you, I always pray with joy..."
—Philippians 1:3-4

A Journey of Faith with the Faithful

James W. Bradley

When I was a child, God came to our congregation every Sunday. I saw him. It took my mother quite awhile to convince me that the man with the snow-white hair, kind face and deep gentle voice was not God. As I have reflected on the influence of persons on my life, I do believe that this early experience helped to shape me as I have continued to *see* God in the lives of others.

"Every time I think of you, I thank my God. And whenever I mention you in my prayers, it makes me happy. This is because you have taken part with me in spreading the good news from the first day you heard it. All of you have helped in the work God has given me..." Philippians 1:3,4,5,7b. This is what Paul was saying to some faithful persons in the church.

Whenever I read this passage and at other times too, memories strengthen and humble me as I reflect on the way persons have touched my life. Who was the most influential person in my life? That would be hard to answer. There have been many persons who have *been there* when sharing was needed most.

When I was a young teen I dealt with the issues most teens do. What will I do with my life? Where should I go to college? Mr. Roy was the church custodian. I remember conversations with this humble man. These conversations usually occurred on the stairs as he *took a break* from his work. I do not remember what he said, but I do remember *he took the time to listen.*

My heart is filled with gratitude for the persons who *have taken the time* to listen and journey with me. Most of the persons who have influenced my life will not have their names mentioned in a book. Many are simple people living in humble residences. These people do have riches that have deeply influenced me. One of the

First Christian Church (1889) - *Narrows, Virginia*

First Christian Church of Narrows, Virginia, was founded in 1889. At that time the church had eighty members. The first church building was started in 1891 and dedicated in 1896. The men, women and first pastor, Rev. Jimmie H. Johnson, did most of the construction work themselves.

In 1957, the present building was constructed due to increased growth and membership. The church is an active member of the Virginia Region of the Christian Church (Disciples of Christ).

beautiful attributes of the people of God is that *we listen.* The journey of faith is in community and consequently the persons in community influence one another.

Recently I have stated several times, "words shape our world." This is not original with me. And as I reflect on this powerful thought I give thanks for you who have spoken words of kindness, encouragement, challenge, rebuke and love. My world has been shaped and continues to be shaped by persons of all walks of life. Allow me to encourage you to be one who *takes the time to listen* to another.

It has been a long time since I walked into that little church in Narrows, Virginia, and *saw God.* I am thankful I have seen God many times since then in the lives of persons like you. Persons have always seen more in me than I have seen in myself. Thank you, church custodian, teacher, pastor, college president, colleague, student, neighbor, friend, parishioners, coaches, players and dear wife and children for allowing me to *see God* with you. I would like to encourage you to continue to *stop and listen.* There just might be a little boy or girl who will see God in you and his or her life will be changed forever.

Anderson University School of Theology, Adam W. Miller Chapel (1975)
Anderson, Indiana

"Though my father and mother forsake me, the LORD will receive me."
—Psalm 27:10

Faith for a Lifetime

Arlene Stevens Hall

ow thrilling it is to hear, read, or observe dramatic testimonies of God's divine action in the lives of men and women, groups, churches, and even nations! My personal testimony is not dramatic, but it reflects a lifelong pilgrimage with the Master. When I was four years old, my mother taught me the verse, *"When my father and mother forsake me, the LORD will take me up."* She was a single parent, struggling with poor health, and concerned about the welfare of her child.

At an early age I chose to follow Jesus Christ as Savior and Lord. That has been a divine friendship through all the joys, sorrows, conflicts, opportunities, and struggles across a lifespan. The Lord never sent a startling vision or spoke in an audible voice, but he has led me step-by-step into a whole array of life experiences. The Psalmist wrote, *"The steps of a good man are ordered by the LORD."* George Mueller, a great Christian who founded orphanages for children, wrote in the margins of his Bible beside that verse, "and the stops too." Both the stops and the starts and the pursuing are all part of the pilgrimage.

Sometimes my husband and I have mused thankfully that two only children with no experience with infants were able to bring two young sons through those early years. We prayed a lot and we often held a son in one arm and a book on parenting in the other. By God's grace we succeeded.

As I entered Christian education ministry, I found myself in a job much bigger than my skills. God was good. He led step-by-step, often through struggle and questions. By his enabling grace and the assistance and patience of many persons, I was able to serve my home congregation joyfully for twenty-four years.

Now these are the sunset years. Who knows what's ahead? A lot of unpleasant things could happen, but I want to envision these years as opportunities to grow, to serve, to experience the living God, my Savior and Friend—to continue the pilgrimage wherever it may lead.

St. Nicholas Lutheran Church (1875)
Peppertown, Indiana

*"And we know that in all things God works for the good of those
who love him, who have been called according to his purpose."*
—Romans 8:28

God's Working

Billie Roy Smith

It was 1943 and I had just turned twenty-five years old. Pearl and I had been married for two and one-half years and our baby daughter, Emma Christie, had recently been born. I was working as a taxi dispatcher for Decatur Transit in Decatur, Alabama. I worked the second shift from three in the afternoon until eleven o'clock at night and handled as many as eight hundred calls on some shifts. There was a lot of stress trying to keep everyone happy.

The United States of America was at war, World War II, "the war to end all wars." My two brothers were already in the service, Howard in the Navy and Doyce in the Army. Since I had been born with the number two and number three vertebrae in my neck fused, a condition that caused my head to move uncontrollably when I walked, I didn't think that I could serve in the military. So I was surprised when on June 1, 1943, I passed the physical and was inducted into the Army. I was given a seven-day furlough and told to report for duty on June 8. Everyone who knew me thought that I would be classified 4-F. So we were in a daze and wondering what would happen next. During the week following my induction I had to try to come to terms with the fact that I was in the Army. I resigned my job and got things in order to the best of my ability. Leaving Pearl and Christie was not easy.

The inductees were sent to Fort McPherson near Atlanta, Georgia, for our assignments. During the two weeks that we were there we had more physical exams and shots. We were issued uniforms and things we would need for basic training. We had some marching drills and classes to help us adjust to military life. For two weeks from early to late we lined up and, among other things, waited. Then we were assigned to our next base. We were taken to the railroad depot and not allowed to call our families. We were told only that we would stay below the Mason and Dixon Line. It was night time

St. Paul's Episcopal Chapel (1902) - *Magnolia Springs, Alabama*

In the late 1800s, Miss Gertrude Smith, a devout Episcopalian from Hinsdale, Illinois, came to Magnolia Springs to care for her mother. She invited a group to her home where she taught Sunday school. In 1901, funds had been collected to build a church. Miss Smith did not get to see the completed church, but always wished to name the church St. Paul's Episcopal Chapel. The Diocesan Bishop, the Right Reverend Robert Wood Barnwell honored her wish and in 1902, St. Paul's Episcopal Chapel was consecrated.

In 1906, St. Paul's Chapel weathered a hurricane, but in 1916 was blown from its foundation by another hurricane. It was replaced with an improved foundation. The chapel seats eighty and the interior is made of heart pine. Above the chancel is a cross of magnolia leaves created by Mrs. Milton Davis. It was hung upon completion of the church in 1902.

and we tried to sleep in our seats. Early in the morning we pulled into the train station and the sign read Petersburg, Virginia. Our destination was Camp Lee, Virginia, a quartermaster training base.

I was assigned to Company D, 13th Quartermaster Training Regiment. My officers were First Lieutenant McNamara, Company Commander, Second Lieutenant Porthouse and Sergeant Courason. These were real Army people and they had a job to do. They tried to be aware of the people in their command and they did a good job. Here, we had more shots and exams to determine where we would be assigned in the Corps. The hot summer months were ahead and the basic training was laid out for thirteen weeks with six weeks of really hard work up front.

During the first weeks of basic training I was assigned to kitchen patrol *(KP)* and at least once to guard duty which was for twenty-four continuous hours. I took part in all the training including an obstacle course and firing a rifle. I remember crawling on my stomach under barbed wire. We had some five mile hikes during which we wore heavy backpacks. The cadre made it as hard on us as they could. During one march I blacked out and fell to the ground. That called for more tests and X-rays. One day at noon I was told to report to the company office and that Lt. McNamara wanted to see me. I was told that I had not done anything wrong but that he wanted to talk to me. I went into his office and saluted. He put me at ease. He told me that he had reviewed my records and X-rays. He said that he did not know how I got inducted considering the condition of my neck. Then he shocked me by saying that he was going to keep me for at least ninety days which would qualify me for the GI Bill of Rights. He said that he couldn't keep me off KP but that I would not be assigned guard duty. He told me that I had been put there unnecessarily and that I deserved some consideration for that.

Time passed. July drifted into August and August dragged into September. It was hot and I was lonely. I wrote letters home and even wrote one letter to Harold Phillips at the Gospel Trumpet Company. His reply was encouraging. I visited the Church of God in Richmond where Melvin Wampler was the pastor. I spent several weekends with Reverend and Mrs. Wampler that summer. I was discharged from the Army on September 24, 1943, with more than enough time served to qualify me for the GI Bill of Rights. I returned to my family and went to work for Ingalls Shipbuilding in the accounting department. I took an accounting course by correspondence from LaSalle Extension School in Chicago.

More time passed and I responded to a call that I had felt very early on in my life, the call to ministry. I had preached my first sermon when I was seventeen. Pearl, Christie and I moved to Fairfax, Alabama, where I pastored the Church of God and worked in the towel factory. After a while we decided to move to Anderson, Indiana, so that I could attend college. As a result of my military service I qualified for the benefits available to all veterans. These benefits paid for my tuition except for one semester and there was also some living expense money available. Pearl worked at Guide Lamp during this time and we shared the care of our daughter. It would have been very difficult, if not impossible, for me to attend college were it not for these benefits. We began to really see how God was working in our lives while we were stewing. I graduated with a Bachelor of Theology degree in June of 1949. Those of us graduating with theology degrees were also ordained at graduation, the last class to be ordained during these ceremonies. It thrills my soul that my ordination certificate is signed by John Morrison, Earl Martin, Adam Miller, and Dale Oldham. If it were not for the *mistake* of my induction into the military it is likely that my diploma and my ordination certificate would never have been placed in my hands. These treasures and my CPA certificate which I earned later have made it possible for our family, which grew to include our son Rick, daughter-in-law Sherry, son-in-law Stan, our grandchildren Hayley, Will, Michael, granddaughter-in-law Heather, and great-grandson Daniel, to have a wonderful life through many difficult and blessed times.

Billie Roy Smith

I have said that if we knew what lies ahead maybe we could plan and enjoy life. Faith and trust in God are hard to come by in times that are unclear to us. Now almost sixty years since my basic training, I reflect on my life and it is evident to me that God does care for His own, for those who trust Him. He is working even when it does not appear to be so. I have learned a lot along the way. It is my desire to trust my life completely to Him, His will and direction. This I believe, *"All things work together for good for those who love God, who are called according to his purpose."* Amen.

"Wait for the LORD; be strong and take heart and wait for the LORD."
—Psalm 27:14

Faith's Crossing Points

Helen Jones Newell

Everyone has faith. It is a gift of God's grace and we have the potential to develop it. Even an infant has faith, a basic trust, that he or she will be fed.

Our faith is shaped by persons, causes, or concerns that have the greatest worth or *God-like* value to us. The dynamics of faith are determined by the object of our faith, the gods of our life—institutions, education, power, science, government, money, self, success, corporations, significant person(s), or God; that is, what or whom we worship or look to for meaning. If we are fully committed to God through Jesus Christ, then ours is a Christian faith.

My life of faith can be described by the analogy of a journey that involves process, action, experiences, starts and stops, variety, humdrum and surprises, yet ever changing.

Childhood experiences shape one's faith. My parents who were Kansas farmers, lived by two basic principles—hard work and a sense of high moral values. Much later I realized how this *do-it-yourself* attitude influenced my understanding of faith. After the death of my brother in the 1936 influenza epidemic, my parents stopped going to the Methodist church altogether.

Several years later mother took us to the Nazarene church, which was very conservative and unbending in their beliefs. Their emphasis was on sin and the need for salvation, but I never saw myself as being sinful. Out of a sense of fear during a typical revival meeting in March, 1939, at the age of thirteen, I asked God to save me from hell. I made a commitment to be a Christian, whatever that meant.

Faith for me during high school and college was expressed by external standards, doing what was morally right, living according to someone else's rules without questioning *why*. Nothing more, nothing less. Yet, there was a desire for something more.

St. John United Church of Christ (1869)
Woodland, Indiana

*Persons interested in forming a new congregation met in the
abandoned Methodist building in 1869 to form St. John
Evangelical Church. Four years later the church bought the
building for $175. In 1892, they bought a half acre of land and
erected a new building. The cornerstone of what is the present
sanctuary was laid on May 29, 1892. Wood burning stoves
provided heat. Light was furnished by many kersoene lamps
mounted on a large wheel which hung from the ceiling. The big
bell cost $117 and was rung on Saturday evening at 6:00
heralding the coming day of rest. Its somber tones also told the
neighborhood of a death with each toll representing a year in the
life of the deceased. After a series of mergers, the congregaton
became part of the United Church of Christ in 1957.*

The Church of God became a new horizon in my faith journey when Arlo and I married. Not only did he become my husband, he was my pastor and continues today to be my mentor. I learned that faith was more than a belief system and *doing* what was correct. However, I continued to question, accepted what I couldn't understand, and allowed God to direct my life.

Faith involves belief, relationship, and action. Beliefs are foundational to faith, but are not an end in themselves. God's gift of faith touches the inner being of a person and disposes one toward a lived relationship of trust and loyalty to a faithful God. The third dimension of Christian faith requires an activity of *doing*, of *being engaged in the world.*

A pivotal point in my faith occurred in 1959. One morning while eating breakfast Eric, our son, complained of a headache. Did this mean surgery again? When I asked if he wanted me to pray, he answered, "You have prayed a hundred times; it hasn't done any good...but pray again." When I randomly picked a scripture for our morning devotions, it was *"Wait for the LORD; be strong and take heart and wait for the LORD." –Psalms 27:14.* Was this actually God's word for me? How was I to wait? I had always taken charge. Arlo was in Europe and it would take two days for him to arrive home. The people of our church became an example of lived faith to me, praying and caring for us.

My journey began as I experienced faith through the lives of others. The need for self-worth and acceptance led me to become part of a faith community. Yet I doubted, questioned, and explored alternatives to earlier understandings until I embraced a personal faith of my own centered on Jesus Christ as Savior and Lord.

Faith is not just knowing about God, it is knowing God in an intimate relationship of love and grace that enables one to reach out to others and then to the world.

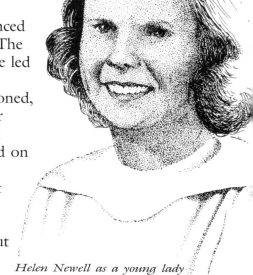

Helen Newell as a young lady

"...'The harvest is plentiful, but the workers are few. Ask the Lord of the harvest, therefore, to send out workers into his harvest field. Go! I am sending you...'"
—Luke 10:2-3

Healing at the Crossroads

John M. Johnson

I was entering my final year of high school. I had long desired to be a missionary, although, honestly, I had no idea what a missionary was supposed to do. A work camp from our church was being formed to go the intersection of the Pan-American Highway and the Trans-Brazilian Highway, a place called *Itituba*. We were going to join with German-speaking Brazilians from the south and Portuguese-speaking persons from the north to help build a church. Always eager for another cross-cultural adventure, I convinced my folks to let me go. I knew the trip would be fun. I knew it would be a lot of work. I also knew I would learn a great deal about myself and missions. What I did not know was that I was traveling toward a major crossroads, an intersection of my life and God's will. By the time I left Brazil I would never think about missions or my involvement in it in the same way again.

We had been at the worksite a few days. It was hot and humid but I was strong and stubborn. Sunday after church while many in our group were resting, I was given the opportunity to go fishing. Who would pass up the opportunity to fish on a tributary of the Amazon?

All afternoon I sat in a small boat in the hot equatorial sun catching nothing. Late that afternoon, back in a shed-like attachment to the missionary's house, stretched out in a hammock, I began to get cold, very cold. It wasn't long before I was miserable. I was diagnosed with sunstroke. My fever continued to rise, going above 105 degrees. The missionaries, Bill and Betty Mottinger, went around the village to find ice. My fever spiked to such an extent that they put a fan at the head and another at the foot of my bed. All night long they covered me in sheets soaked in ice water. A day or so later when my fever broke it went subnormal, equally dangerous, I understand. A telegram was sent saying that I was very sick and that I might have to be

Ain Kfarzabad Church of God (1962) - *Ain Kfarzabad, Lebanon*

The church in Ain Kfarabad was started as a home ministry in 1962 by Sleiman Aara. In 1982, Sunday morning services officially began in a rented facility. In 1991, the current building was erected.

Today, in addition to the regular Sunday morning and evening services held in that building, Pastor Touma Mina is leading several home ministry meetings in neighboring villages.

Ain Kfarzabad is a mixed village consisting of half Christian Orthodox and half Muslim Shiites. The villages of the Bekaa Valley where it is located are mostly inhabited by Muslims.

evacuated. Each evening, all night long, the German-speaking group would gather to pray for me. I learned later that they would come to the mission house each morning and ask if I was ready to work.

For me, the days passed slowly. In the afternoon of that third day after I became ill the work campers went to watch a soccer match in the city. I was left at home with one other person. I had begun to feel a bit better but I still had no energy. I was feeling sorry for myself and complaining about my situation. It was then that God spoke to me. It wasn't audible but it was clearly God. "So you think you want to be a missionary?" He asked me. "It's not what you think it will be." And then, a pause. Again, "Are you sure you still want to be a missionary?"

It seems that God wanted me to come face-to-face with the fact that missions was more than a cross-cultural adventure. It was more than physical labor in another place. It was a struggle, a spiritual battle. I became aware that being involved in this calling would cost me everything. I clearly remember responding out loud, "Yes, Lord, I want to be a missionary!"

As I look back, I believe that my full physical healing happened at that moment. By the next day, much to the chagrin of Betty Mottinger, herself a nurse, I was back at the worksite physically doing more than I had ever done before. People from the village gathered around to see the one who had been so sick with a fever pushing loads of concrete up a ramp to the second floor of the church building.

Before leaving Brazil, Betty Mottinger cautioned me to have a full medical check-up upon my return to the States. "It is possible that you might have some sort of a relapse," she warned. Shortly after I returned to the States, I did indeed visit my family doctor. Hearing my story he ran some blood tests. The verdict, in the words of the doctor, was, "I don't doubt that you were sick, but according to these tests, it was as if it never happened."

Over nearly twenty years of missionary service Gwen and I have faced many difficulties. Missionary life has not always been easy for us. That certainly is the case now that we are working in the Middle East. Regardless of the circumstance or location, we have always felt God's presence, His equipping, His healing, His encouraging. Time and again I remember God's question and His healing at the crossroads in Brazil, indeed a crossroads in my life.

*"By faith we understand that the universe was formed at God's command,
so that what is seen was not made out of what was visible."*
—Hebrews 11:3

Fork in the Road

Harold L. Phillips

Yogi Berra is credited with saying: "When you come to a fork in the road, take it!" My problem in the summer of 1936 was that there were four forks in the road and I did not know which to take. During college years I had worked part-time at the *San Diego Sun* and had gotten a taste for printer's ink and publication. This was followed in my last year by a job as a courtesy driver for Ford Motor Company at the California-Pacific Exposition in San Diego. Graduation day came in June and I was plunged into a struggle over which fork in the road to take. Here is what they were:

First, an invitation to continue working for Ford Motor Company. A Ford executive urged me to take this opportunity.

Second, an opportunity to begin graduate studies at the University of California with guarantee of a teaching fellowship that would see me through to a Ph.D. My major professor offered to open that door for me.

Third, an offer to become a field organizer for the University Bible Clubs organization and be active on many university and college campuses. I had been president of the San Diego State College chapter for several years. An executive of that organization urged that decision.

Fourth, my pastor, Albert Kempin, recommended that I journey to Anderson, Indiana, and begin biblical and theological training at Anderson College and Theological Seminary. I was wrestling with some sense of that *call* but did not want to forgo some aspect of journalism.

The struggle was fierce for a while. The printer's ink and the yen to write kept asserting themselves and at that time I did not envision any way those could be mated to a call to ministry. But eventually the die was cast. I would go to Anderson and whatever opened there for me.

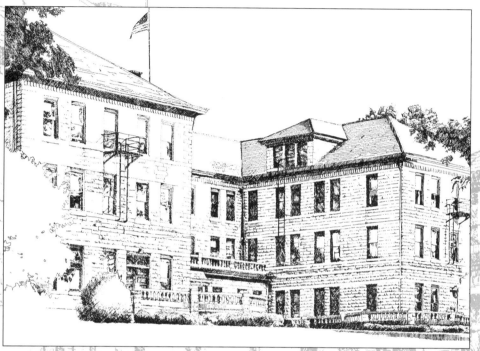

Old Main, Anderson College (1906-1968) - *Anderson, Indiana*

   Old Main construction was begun in 1905 by the workers of the Gospel Trumpet Company to provide housing for their families. Timbers came from the St. Louis World's Fair. Building blocks were made by hand on the site. It became the birthplace of Anderson College in 1917, providing offices, classrooms, laboratories, living quarters for the faculty and students, a chapel, library, laundry, dining room and post office. It was replaced in 1970 by Decker Hall.

In the blistering heat of August, 1936, this prospective student for Anderson College and Theological Seminary arrived at the Pennsylvania depot. He lugged his footlocker suitcase out through Park Place to the south door of Old Main and entered. Old mattresses and bed springs were propped up against the wall. A few bare-bulbed light fixtures hung from the ceiling. The odor of rotting cabbage hung in the air.

I said out loud the first thing that came to mind (and please forgive the language): "My God, what have I done!" I had come from an almost new campus dotted with beautiful white buildings with red-tiled roofs, Spanish architecture. For a moment I was almost overcome with disillusionment.

But school got underway and this new student was assigned to an outside-work crew at the rate of twenty-five cents an hour, tuition credit. My wages at Ford had been more than double that plus perks. First assignment for the crew was tearing out the cement foundations of what had once been a barn. One day a messenger came from across the street at the Gospel Trumpet Company looking for "Harold Phillips." It appeared that the General Manager,

Harold L. Phillips - 1950

whom I had met that summer at a youth convention in Los Angeles, was wanting me to report to his office.

To make a long story short, I was offered employment in the editorial department of that religious publishing house. Retirement came after forty years of a very satisfying career in religious journalism. The printer's ink, the yen to write and ministerial call melded into one—and all because of a fork in the road that seemed at the time to be most unlikely.

All this might seem to be just luck. But another way to look at it is to see it as an unlikely fork in the road—but one taken by faith.

*"Making request, if by any means now at length I might have
a prosperous journey by the will of God to come unto you."*
—Romans 1:10

Tapestry

Christina Tellechea Accornero

The best place for me to reflect on and think about my faith journey is on a beach somewhere near the crashing waves of the ocean. It is so wonderful to be near the big waves that collide with the shore, almost as if they were struggling to get past the cliffs, rocks, or sandy beach. I really do think the ocean fights with the coastline and keeps beating against it to find an open door through which it can spread out and once again become peaceful. Maybe that is why I like being so near—to hear and feel the struggle as well as sense that the calm comes with the ebb and flow of the tide.

It also seems that the ocean has become the image, the metaphor, for me in my attempt to describe a faith journey of some twenty-five years. It has been a journey of ebbs and flows, struggles and peaceful places, disappointments and dreams. It even began near the ocean in Santa Barbara, California. I prayed to ask Christ into my life, just after finishing a wonderful lobster dinner with a good friend. I still remember the great sunset and calm ocean that evening—a peaceful beginning to a wild ride!

The ride, the journey, with Jesus to this point has been wild in the sense that it has been a *full speed ahead* kind of run and not a walk. It seems that I have been trying to take it all in and learn as much as I can, as fast as I can. After all, I have had to make up for the first twenty-five years without a relationship with God! When you grow up as an atheist, believing that God doesn't even exist, it is a major change to go from *no Jesus* at all to *give it all to Jesus* overnight. I went from an angry, bitter, disappointed person to one who said, "Wow, someone really loves me that much!" I don't think it was the lobster dinner or the sunset either, even though that helped!

I grew up as a Mexican/Italian kid on the streets of Los Angeles. Although it was not as tough a city in the 1950s and 1960s as it is

Trinity Episcopal Church (1821) - St. Augustine, Florida

Trinity Episcopal Church was established by missionaries and
struggled along until the Revolutionary War. After treaties were
signed and the church was under Spanish dominance, the church was
abolished. In 1789, the Anglicans requested missionary services from
the newly-formed Protestant Episcopal Church of the United States.

On October 6, 1821, Rev. Andrew Fowler conducted the first
Episcopal services in St. Augustine, Florida. The church building was
erected in 1830. This parish grew until the Civil War when it fell
upon hard times, but gradually did succeed. The women of the church
helped greatly in raising monies for stained-glass windows, an organ,
and a steeple with a bell by holding bazaars, fairs and teas. The
church continues to be a thriving parish involved in its community.

now, I learned early on that survival skills were very important. My parents taught me to stand up tall and to be proud of my ethnic and cultural heritage, as well as how to appreciate those from other diverse backgrounds. Those first twenty-five years of life were foundational in building my worldview and giving me a sense of the wonder, diversity, and beauty of the world community.

I can't imagine my life as a Christian without having lived those first years as a non-believer in a mega-city like Los Angeles. I was taught early on to be comfortable with people of all colors, sizes, shapes, languages, and cultures. Since becoming a Christian, I have appreciated the fullness of God's creation so much more because of that early introduction. It is my passion these days to help others see what a wonderfully diverse world God has given us. My hope for the future is that the boundless community of God's people will learn to worship together, embrace each other, and love each other. My faith journey thus far would have been so devoid of joy and love had it not been for the great variety of people that God has sent my way. Like a beautiful tapestry of many colors, God has woven a special world for me that crosses all boundaries of race, ethnicity, language, culture, and religion. I am so rich!

"And we know that in all things God works for the good of those who love him, who have been called according to his purpose."
—Romans 8:28

A Caring Faith

Walter R. Gatton

My journey of faith led me through forty-two years in the full-time pastoral ministry. I was unsure about how to retire. Would I slow down to a passive quiet life of resting and golf? Since I had relatively good health I offered myself to part-time ministry. I responded to a call from White Chapel Church of God. Then came a dramatic turn...my life has opened up.

Drawing upon my experiences as a pastor, my life has opened up to a new and exciting adventure in pastoral care. Now, for over fourteen years, I have been serving here in South Daytona, Florida. I try to set an example of what it means to *care*, with my attitude, my influence and my hugs. I was privileged to do those things I valued the highest.

Prayer to my Lord is vital and important! God is moved upon His throne by the hurting souls brought to Him by the corporate prayers of His caring people. Jesus was moved to *tears* by those who were troubled and in pain. He came with compassion and healing.

My work has brought to me joy, fulfillment and a sense of satifaction, often leading me to stand on the very threshold of eternity. I am priviledged to offer encouragement and hope in Christ our Lord. It is my joy to offer myself and my Lord to those who have pressing needs and hurts. I also try to be alert to those hidden burdens they may be carrying. I stand ready to listen, showing understanding and response to the many needs that God's spirit brings to my attention. I am still learning how to love and to identify with people.

Eileen, my life partner, and I celebrated fifty-nine years of marriage. By the miracle of God's grace she is experiencing good days of renewed health. We are happy for every day our Lord gives us.

The best of my heart says, "I really do care!"

First Church of God (1924) - *New Boston, Ohio*

In 1924, a few people began to meet for prayer meetings in homes. They had been brought together through reading the Gospel Trumpet. Steady growth resulted in the need for a building for regular services. The first building was a store room rented on Gallia Street. Soon after, the members voted to purchase this building. Tent meetings were held in the area and many souls were added to the Church.

In 1952, the building had been condemned and plans for a new building were presented and accepted. Ground was broken on Easter Sunday in 1953. The new building was dedicated on December 11, 1955, with Dr. Eugene Newberry giving the address.

Rev. Walter Gatton pastored this congregation from 1949 to 1952.

"...May people ever pray for him and bless him all day long."
—*Psalm 72:15*

Confidence in Prayer

Robert A. Nicholson

I have been aware of the impact of prayer on my life virtually all of my days. At age five I survived a ruptured appendix. I was not seen by a doctor for twenty-four hours, in the days when no *miracle drugs* were known or available. I have known that my parents' and grandparents' prayers were powerful. At age sixteen, when I traveled six hundred miles from home to enter Anderson College, I knew my parents prayed for me daily. My home congregation, in St. Paul Park, Minnesota, provided daily prayer support—I knew that.

But there was one focal period when the awareness of prayer buoying me up was as real as anything of my life. I had been elected president of Anderson College, which became Anderson University a few years later, and had a period of twelve months as president-elect. A month or two before I actually became president on July 1, 1983, I became aware in my inner spirit of a prayer support which I had never before experienced. Then I began to receive letters saying, "We are praying for you and the college." I did not even know many of the alumni and friends who were writing. Perhaps they merely were bemoaning the retirement of long-term President Robert H. Reardon; but I think not. Rather, they cared deeply about the college and students, and chose to focus that concern on the president, as a personification of the institution.

In any case, it was real, very real. I chose to share my awareness with faculty, staff and students, for whom many of the prayers in reality were being offered; I wanted them to know of the enormous affection, love and concern which surrounded all of us. This was a facet of the role of president which I never had expected. Prayer brings confidence; it makes real the Christian community in which we exist; it brings a buoyancy to lift one in the heavy, burdened times. It truly *enables*, in the Divine sense.

We are privileged to be able to pray for others. God's presence is real and sustaining. We never should forget it.

First Presbyterian Church (1851) - *Anderson, Indiana*

Reverend Edward Scofield organized the First Presbyterian Church in Anderson, Indiana, on September 14, 1851. The railroad came to Anderson that same year. The congregation met in the county courthouse until the first small frame sanctuary was built on the west side of Meridian Street between Tenth and Eleventh.

Later this building was replaced with a brick structure on the same site. This in turn was superceded by a large brick building at the corner of Ninth and Jackson Streets. That building was sold to the I.O.O.F. at the time the church moved into the present location at Tenth and Jackson Streets in 1906.

"What good is it, my brothers, if a man claims to have faith but has no deeds?
In the same way, faith by itself, if it is not accompanied by action, is dead."
—James 2:14,17

Cry of My Heart

Don Deena Johnson

Lord of my heart, there're children cryin'
On city streets, alone, in pain.
They sell themselves for bread or shelter
And no one asks, "What is your name?"
Lord, fan the flame of my compassion.
Unstop my ears, I want to hear.
Peel back the scales and heal my blindness.
Lord of my heart, burn love in me.

Lord of my mind, there're children seekin'
For words of truth to set them free.
But lies seduce and false hopes capture
Oh who will say, "Here is the key"?
Lord, break my will that I may know you.
Confront my lazy intellect.
Do not destroy for lack of knowledge.
Lord of my mind, speak truth through me.

Lord of my soul, there're children hopin'
For justice, peace and family.
They wake each day and watch for springtime.
Will someone smile, "Child, come with me"?
Lord, breathe in me your breath of goodness.
Infill my spirit with your grace
'Till ev'ry stranger is my neighbor,
Lord of my soul, breathe peace through me.

Come gather 'round you little children.
There will be no more cryin' here
'Cause Jesus is the truth I'm livin'
Lord of my all, You're light in me.

Dedicated to Adrienne Holmes, pastor and friend of children.
(Can be sung to the tune, "Wayfarin' Stranger")

St. Joseph Catholic Church
Stockbridge, Massachusetts

"...we have not stopped praying for you and asking God to fill you with the knowledge of his will through all spiritual wisdom and understanding."
—Colossians 1:9

One Simple Conversation

James L. Edwards

nowing and doing the will of God has been a lifetime quest for most followers of Jesus. I have always believed that by God's choosing, we know most of what God wants to speak to us through the scriptures and through people. I have never heard an audible voice and have doubted those whose experiences have been otherwise. Even those winsome college students whom I love often speak of what God has told them to do. I accept it as their perception, but doubt if their ears were involved, so much as were their inner hearts and spirits.

A turning point came in my life when, as a young pastor, I had a conversation with Robert Reardon. In my days as a young staff member at Anderson College, I never reported directly to this impressive man who served for twenty-five years as the second president of the college. I always felt he was interested in my life and my work. He never hesitated to call me into his office or to take me along on advancement calls. I was one of many who could point to him as a mentor in leadership.

We were together at a pastors' conference and President Reardon became rather restless with the group process being introduced. So he invited me aside for a chat. He asked me what I really wanted to accomplish with my life. I told him I have had a love all my life with learning, and thought that surely someday I would again be involved in a ministry of Higher Education. It was as close as I was willing to come in telling him that one day, I thought I might be called upon to follow in his footsteps to serve again in one of the church's colleges.

He then told me his thoughts about such a future. Dr. Reardon said the person who would one day follow him would likely be a pastor who had successfully led a growing church. He said such a person would have acquired an earned doctorate in something, and

First Church of God (1913) - *Piqua, Ohio*

The first group of families began worshiping together in 1913, and the first building was contructed on Cherry Street in the 1920s. In 1926, the building on Madison Avenue was purchased and under the leadership of J. H. Edwards an education unit was added. Architect, John S. Kane, designed the new sanctuary and added a narthex. On May 20, 1956, the "new" church was dedicated with Dr. Dale Oldham as the speaker.

The first Headstart Program in Piqua, Ohio, was started in this church in the 1970s.

would have a strong, devoted family life. These three things would be a major accomplishment for anyone who was serious about leading one of the church's colleges. Grow a church, get a doctorate, and nurture a wonderful family. It was as though I had an assignment from God. He never spoke with me again about his thoughts on the presidency of the college, nor about my own ministry. I never asked his views again. He was probably speaking in broad generalities and not necessarily about my future. But that was the moment I began a quest to honor a call of God should it ever come.

The journey was a challenge. I found myself in pastoral leadership in a dynamic, rapidly-growing congregation. The church was exploding in development just at the time when I was beginning doctoral studies; a period in which I seemed to have the least to give. My family was first priority, but without the devoted efforts of companion Deanna, we could have grown apart and I could have missed the best of my children's growing years.

That one simple conversation of some thirty or forty minutes with a mentor and model, had taken on a clear tone of an assignment that set the course of my life for the next fourteen years. Long after it seemed the college would look my way for leadership, I was on task. Lincoln once said, "I will prepare, and perhaps someday the opportunity will come." It was the word of a wise mentor who set my path to all I am doing today.

"Therefore, since we have been justified through faith,
we have peace with God through our Lord Jesus Christ."
—Romans 5:1

A Haven of Rest

James A. Albrecht

etty and I, and our three teen-age children had been in Cairo for nearly a year. Crowded into a massive Middle Eastern culture, coping with teen-agers in school, adjusting to strange sounds and smells, life became very frustrating for me. Imagine trying to learn Arabic at age forty-eight? My head felt like it was filled with concrete. More than once, I questioned God, "Are you sure I didn't mistake your call for my own ambitious delusions." God was slow to answer, allowing me time to discover the answer for myself.

The one oasis in the desert of life was the Maadi Community Church. Founded by the Anglican Church when the British controlled Egypt, it was built after the classic village tradition. Appropriately named The Church of St. John the Baptist, it was a landmark for foreigners of many nationalities living in Egypt.

As Egyptian nationalism forced most of the British to leave the country, Wilbur and Evelyn Skaggs began their missionary work. They served from 1945 until 1958. St. John's Church had few people and no Sunday worship. Wilbur asked permission to open the church for use of the international community of a few hundred people at that time. He served as the initial pastor and the church was a beacon of hope in the midst of revolution and social turmoil. In later years, Wilbur came back as an interim pastor at a time when the church was overflowing with expatriates from around the world, and refugees from war-torn Sudan.

Back to my story. One Friday I went to worship with our family. The pastor, David Johnson, a Lutheran from Wisconsin, saw that I was having second thoughts about being in Egypt. He said, "Don't look back, Jim!" Those words were a turning point for me. I began to realize that God had work for me to do, that these trying days were the prelude to effective ministry among our struggling Egyptian churches.

Maadi Community Church (1930) - *Cairo, Egypt*

The sanctuary was first built as the Episcopal (Anglican) Church of St. John the Baptist. A periodic Sunday morning community service, largely attended by the American community, grew out of the St. John's fellowship. This group developed into the present Maadi Community Church.

Each week, our family joined other devout Christians from many denominations in common worship of Christ the Lord. We sang the hymns of faith, heard words of encouragement, and received spiritual fortification for our life in a foreign culture. And our fellowship and conversation with English-speaking friends renewed our spirits and gave us a touch of home.

The Maadi Community Church today serves multiple congregations of some one thousand persons each week from many nations, including an African refugee community. Our two daughters and four grandsons who live in Egypt now count it their church. This is indeed a House of Prayer for all people and a haven of rest for many.

I'll Follow with Rejoicing

Charles W. Naylor, 1874-1950   Andrew L. Byers, 1870-1952

1. The future lies unseen ahead, It holds I know not what;
2. Doth he not know what I shall meet Upon life's rugged way?
3. No matter how things look to me, Nor if they threaten sore;
4. The glory of eternal dawn Shines from his smiling face;

But still I know I need not dread, For Jesus faileth not.
Will he not guide my halting feet, Lest from the path I stray?
I know my way prepared shall be, For Christ leads on before.
So trusting him I follow on, With heart made strong by grace.

CHORUS

I'll follow him with rejoicing, With rejoicing, rejoicing;
I'll follow him, I'll follow him, With rejoicing I will follow him;

I know he safely will lead me To my eternal home.
I know he safely will lead me on

"My purpose is that they may be encouraged in heart..."
—Colossians 2:2

My Sister's House

Christy Spaulding Boyer

Upstairs, I rest
In bright winter light
My sister's hands, tiny and translucent,
slide a blue glazed plate
of salad, fish, and fries,
once frozen, now cooked, warm and crisp,
a fork, a knife, a napkin
a tall glass of water makes patterns
across a wooden tray
Peace is a blanket across me.
Crisis is cold and waits
outside in November air.
What will fish taste like?
Its scent of breading
coats my nostrils.
I chew slowly with meaning.
A fish, silver and pink, swam
joyously free, Alive,
in cool river water.
Now it flows
through my veins
and fills the emptiness
between my ribs.
A simple meal, she says.
My shirt is suddenly wet,
milk spreads like black
ink on white paper.
I laugh, then cry without sound,
tears, layer upon recent tears to
parch my cheeks as snow melts
in the sun to thicken an icicle.
I pity the sweetness of my body

St. Philip Catholic Church (1841) - *Franklin, Tennessee*

Missionaries had preached in the town of Franklin since 1821. In 1847, Bishop Miles purchased land for the purpose of building a church. He paid $400 in gold. Although the building was not completed until 1871, the first record of Mass in the town was in 1841. Bishop Bryne declared St. Philip a parish in 1898.

The year 1973 was marked by rapid parish growth. An all-purpose building was designed to be functional for Sunday worship as well as religious education. The new Parish Center was dedicated in July, 1975.

Naive, as a good-hearted child
arms outstretched with an
unwanted gift.
How can I tell it the baby
cannot nurse?
My sister's eyes come to me, bluer,
Her smile, tender, small,
Knowing strength runs from her
deep veins and out
as she feeds me the substance
of her love,
all from the life
she has been joyfully swimming.

Clay Boyer

"...The body is not meant for sexual immorality,
but for the Lord, and the Lord for the body."
—1 Corinthians 6:13

A Career Changing Encounter

Paul A. Tanner

The date was November, 1983. The place was Cincinnati, Ohio. My background included thirteen years in pastoral ministry and twenty-four years as a national church executive. The encounter was with Dr. Jerry Kirk, pastor of the College Hill Presbyterian Church, one of the most godly persons to ever cross my path.

A few months earlier, while participating in a meeting with denominational executives, an invitation came to attend the first National Consultation on Pornography. Most of these executives did attend. Thirty-seven years in the ministry, and never before had I heard a message on pornography and the church's responsibility to do something about it.

The church has been called by Christ to penetrate society as light and salt. But the silence of 300,000 pulpits caused the pornographers to think that we didn't see it, or if we did, that we didn't care. Our silence was taken for tolerance or approval.

The big shock was not to learn that X-rated bookstores were attracting young males, with graphic pictures of nude women. What did shock me was to learn how many children were being robbed of their innocence, at a very tender age. I was grieved to hear how a multi-million dollar sex industry was devouring our children, devastating our women and destroying our families.

The entertainment industry had taken us from silent movies downtown to hard-core downstairs. With modern technology, a sewer had broken loose and was spewing its filth down every street in America, and right into our homes.

As a church executive, my platter was already too full. Any involvement on my part could be made possible only by putting more hours in the day, and more days in the week. I was enraged and

First Congregational Church (1857) - *Indianapolis, Indiana*

Plymouth Congregational Church was organized on August 9, 1857, with thirty-one charter members. For two years it met in the Senate Chambers of the old State House. The first building was erected on the northwest corner of the Circle, opposite Christ Episcopal Church, and was dedicated on February 24, 1867. In January, 1884, a new building at Meridian and New York Streets was dedicated. The U.S. government wanted the site for a Federal Building so the congregation moved again, this time to 14th Street and Central Avenue.

Over the years several smaller Congregational churches merged and eventually First Congregational Church was established on Pennsylvania, north of 71st Street. After several denominational mergers the congregation became a part of the United Church of Christ.

determined not to sit idly by and watch this devastation take place.

Upon returning to Anderson, I marched directly into city hall to confront our mayor about the three adult book stores in our town. Soon I had on board the pastors, the city council, the chief of police and the county prosecutor.

I became a fervent activist. I took a sabbatical leave to work directly with Jerry Kirk. I spearheaded the move to have the Church of God General Assembly pass major resolutions on pornography. I founded a city-wide action group, Citizens for Community Values. The three bookstores were shut down, pronto.

Rome fell while moralists were asleep, and I could not sleep. I crisscrossed the country, speaking hundreds of times in colleges, church headquarters, civic clubs, ministers' meetings and every place the door was open.

It haunted me to think that some day one of my kids or grandkids might look into my casket and say, "He knew about the ravages of sexual perversion, but chose to do nothing about it."

The unity I had taught for many years became an exciting reality, as I sat in the home of the Roman Catholic Cardinal, John O'Connor, along with the heads of twenty-six inter-faith groups, and helped found the Religious Alliance Against Pornography, which remains active to this day.

Every child who has been spared the death of innocence, every girl who has escaped molestation or rape, every young man who has been rescued from his addiction, and every home that has been restored is sufficient reward.

Pornography is still alive and well. It is more accessible, more acceptable, more anonymous (promoted by respected corporations) and more addictive than ever before.

We dare not let the salt lose its savor. People of faith must seize the initiative and become agents of change. New voices are needed, everywhere, to speak up and say, "enough is enough."

"...'Speak, LORD, for your servant is listening...'"
—1 Samuel 3:9

A Call to Ministry

Dwight L. Grubbs

ow do people become pastors? The paths are many and varied, but let me tell my story.

My father became a pastor at the tender age of eighteen and served without interruption until he was seventy-four. He always seemed to enjoy what he was doing. As a child, I admired him and looked forward to the time when I would become a pastor. I grew up with the understanding that God called those whom He wanted in the ministry. And when God called, it would be clear and compelling.

When I was about fourteen, the Cypress Street Church of God in West Monroe, Louisiana, built a new building and I was employed as janitor. The inside walls had not been finished so there were bare two-by-fours and sheetrock. One Saturday, when I was eating my lunch in the junior boys classroom, I wrote a note to God. Between the two-by-fours, I wrote: "God, should you choose to call me into ministry, I am available." I so enjoyed just being in a church building, that I prayed to be allowed to spend my life there!

In the meantime, I explored my interest in forestry, medical missions and teaching. But I did not feel *called* to anything in particular.

For reasons I do not understand, my call did not become clear until nine years later. On Saturday morning, November 11, 1956, I knelt by my footlocker in the barracks at Fort Carson, Colorado, and dedicated my life to God for the Christian ministry. I felt called.

Prior to that morning, I had been seeking for clarity and direction. I read books, wrote many letters, and talked with several people, especially Dad. I was not resisting, just making sure.

After forty-five years as a pastor and teacher of pastors, I still get a special feeling when I enter a sanctuary. I feel at home and safe in a church building. It has been a joy to have made my living doing just what I wanted to do—hanging out at the church!

Cypress Street Church of God (1941) - *West Monroe, Louisiana*

The Cypress Street Church of God held its first worship service on Easter Sunday morning, 1941, in the home of A. B. Mizell in Monroe, Louisiana. The congregation moved to a store building and later to a school. Under the leadership of T. E. Miller, a house on South Second Street was purchased and renovated to become a chapel and parsonage.

In the fall of 1944, J. C. Grubbs moved, with his family, from South Carolina to become the pastor. The congregation decided to relocate to Cypress Street because most of the people lived in West Monroe. In the summer of 1947, the first unit of the building was completed with the pastor and volunteer labor doing most of the work. Since then, two major additions and renovations have been completed and the congregation continues to thrive.

"Then my soul will rejoice in the LORD and delight in his salvation."
—Psalm 35:9

It Is Well with My Soul

Risë Wood Singer

One life impacts another for all eternity. I was only eighteen when Mrs. Troutman came into my life. That was over thirty years ago now. Her husband was my first *real* boss and we all three became instant friends.

After Mr. Troutman died with a cancerous brain tumor, I began to spend more time with her. Mrs. T. and I shared a mutual love for many things including, great old hymns, puppy dogs and Wendy's chili. Her wisdom and patience became invaluable to me. She prayed daily for me and I depended on those prayers.

A year after Mr. Troutman's death, Mrs. T. had a heart attack and a stroke, which left her body partially disabled. Through therapy and determination, she was able to stay in her home. I assumed the responsibilities of her care. My visits became more regular until I was there every day. She was my purpose!

I remember one specific occasion when her prayers saved my life. I was traveling on a two-lane state highway to Wabash, Indiana, to visit a friend. Suddenly a semi appeared behind me and was trying to run over me. I was going *a hundred miles an hour,* but I was not getting ahead of him. Miraculously, as we approached an intersection, the semi backed off. I drove on to Wabash safely, although shaken.

When I got to Mrs. T.'s house that afternoon, she said, before I could tell her what happened, "I had an overwhelming feeling this morning that you were dead." I said, "What did you do?" She said, "I prayed that you would not be dead and that you would be safe." The semi had backed off while she was praying!

God used her in mighty ways during the six years she endured her incapacitated body. My Mrs. T. died in May, 2001, but her faith and influence will live on in me. Her birthday was December 21st, and on the calendar page for that day was written, "One of the most helpful ways to dig deeper into your life is to expose yourself to people of faith, people who are farther along the journey than you are."

It Is Well With My Soul is her legacy. So may it be mine!

Pleasant Street Free Baptist Church (1829)
Springvale, Maine

This church was established following a powerful revival in Shapleigh, Maine, in 1829. The building was built in the 1860s.

"However, do not rejoice that the spirits submit to you,
but rejoice that your names are written in heaven."
—Luke 10:20

When Faith Became Sight

Charles N. Moore

To my dying day, I will believe that somehow Ray was given the privilege of seeing the light of heaven. This took place several hours before his death. This *seeing the light of heaven* was so exceedingly important to Ray that he used sources of strength that were most extraordinary to convey the message to me. He could not sing but he, with excruciating effort, tried to sing words from three songs that contained the words *I know.*

Ray never spoke more than several sentences as I greeted him after worship. He never served on a board or committee. However, he was extremely loyal and dependable.

Also he never became outwardly emotional about his walk with Christ, except for a few brief seconds when he silently knelt at the far end of the church altar and truly accepted Christ into his heart. For over forty years he had been faithful in church attendance and had given of his time, as well as his money.

One day I was overwhelmed with work. My pastoral duties list seemed endless, especially since I was the senior pastor and the youth director. I desperately needed someone to set up everything for the youth wiener roast at 6:00 P.M. I could always depend upon Ray. He interrupted his demanding farm work to set up tables, chairs, recreation equipment and bring several grills in his truck.

Around 4:00 P.M. he knocked softly on my study door and told me everything was ready. He emphasized "everything." "Everything?" I asked. "Yes, you will find all the food, paper goods and everything else in the fellowship hall and everything set up on the lawn." I could not believe it. There was an abundance of potato salad, baked beans, pickles, chips, cookies, wieners, buns and all the other special goodies. He would not let me pay for it.

142

First Church of God (1939) - *Elizabethton, Tennessee*

The Elizabethton Church was begun as a Home Missions project of Tacoma Church of God in Johnson City. In March, 1939, a small group met in a home and organized the church. The first services were held in the City Hall building. The lots on which the present church is located were purchased from the city of Elizabethton and the first building was dedicated on June 21, 1941.

Early pastors included Woodrow Starkey, John L. Hicks, William C. Livingston, E. A. Hoffman, M. A. Monday, O. D. Bailey and Charles N. Moore.

Everyone was shocked when a large tumor formed in his stomach. His condition was terminal.

At 3:00 A.M. Ray was urgently calling for me to come to the hospital. I ran in, lifted the oxygen tent surrounding Ray. I listened intently to his weak voice. He was singing over and over again, "I know, I know, I know!"

"Ray, I asked, what do you know?" Turning his head toward the ceiling he very slowly answered, "There is a light there. You will be seen by the light. You must all be there."

With unbelievable effort he tried to touch the pencil in my shirt pocket. I grabbed paper and waited.

With impossible effort he muttered names. I wrote several pages of names. He would pause and breathe hard for as much as a minute and then begin again.

The little church building seated 125 including choir seats. The beautiful stained-glass windows would open. Groups of people huddled around those windows when there was no room inside during Ray's memorial celebration. Ray's three sentences formed the three-point message which he had urgently given with his dying breaths. As the list of names was read, there was sobbing, words of shock and cries of repentance inside and outside the church.

Never had I experienced so much realization of the truth of the words of *I Know Whom I Have Believed* and *I Know My Name Is There*, as I did that day.

"...because I know whom I have believed, and am convinced that he is able to guard what I have entrusted to him for that day."
—2 Timothy 1:12

"O LORD, you are my God; I will exalt you and praise your name, for in perfect faithfulness you have done marvelous things, things planned long ago."
—Isaiah 25:1

God's Faithfulness Never Fails

James W. Lewis

I wanted to be a *success*. Didn't I deserve this for years of study? I seemed on track for success, while living in Houston, Texas. When our family visited in-laws one weekend in 1976, I met a former college friend. He shared with me the tremendous change that had occurred in his life. He indicated that he met some *special* people—called *saints*. I learned that he had *gotten saved*. Through his sharing scriptures of God's great love and forgiveness with me, I began to examine my life in an exciting new way.

When Sunday arrived, we attended this congregation, located in a sleepy town of fifteen hundred. It was a neat, white-framed church huddled near Highway 36. The Somerville Church of God was not a large congregation, but a vibrant one. In it we heard dynamic singing, whose words and tunes touched the depths of our souls as never before. We heard a simple proclamation of the gospel. For us that day, it sounded like *good news*. We accepted Jesus Christ as our Savior and Lord. New life had begun!

Still another milestone was reached in 1980. I accepted a call to ministry. Now our lives would really change! The old vision of success gave way to another. I learned that a call to ministry comes with a call to equip for ministry. When my career as a corporate auditor seemed brightest, the call to equip appeared strongest. I ached for more understanding of the Christian life. However, I kept the yearning at bay because of my family obligations. Yet God threatened to upset our life anyway. I still held back and made excuses, but God's call to prepare never ceased in intensity. "Well, as soon as I get everything together, I will go to seminary." This was my typical response in those days. I soon learned that anything less than faith does not please God. All my

Somerville Church of God (1948) - *Somerville, Texas*

*The Somerville Church of God was organized in 1948
and since then it has mothered two other churches.*

efforts and plans never seemed to work. Only when we agreed with God that moving out by faith is the only way forward, did we find true peace and courage for the future. The Spirit of God ministered *assurance* to our souls. In August, 1982, we left our jobs and moved weeks later to Southwestern Baptist Theological Seminary in Fort Worth, Texas.

Upon arrival there, we had only enough money for several weeks living expenses. Further, we both had no jobs and I did not even have money for my first semester in seminary. What had we done? Did we hear God correctly? Was it even God we heard? There were some family members so upset with our *irresponsible* behavior that they made it clear we were terrible parents. One indicated that our two children needed to be removed from our care.

Good News! We *had* to depend on God and God's people as never before. All along the journey, God provided miracle upon miracle—all so undeserved. From seminary in Texas to Ph.D. work at Duke University in Durham, North Carolina, God again called me to further work to equip for ministry. The same story line can be repeated! Again, we have testimony upon glorious testimony of God's faithfulness toward us. Now our greatest testimony, twenty-five years later, is the peace of knowing that we are still in the will of God. God led us from that Sunday morning in a small, white-framed, building church to this day on the campus of Anderson University. While God is not through yet, I am confident that God will complete the good work that he has begun. If God calls you to ministry or to do anything, God is ready and willing, with you and others, to see you through! Hallelujah!

"...go to the land I will show you."
—Genesis 12:1

Journey of Faith

Laura Benson Withrow

Houses of worship are amazing to me for they take so many forms. I have worshipped in little, white country churches, in open-sided tabernacles, in the living room of my parents as a part of a new church plant, in a tent for a revival, in small, cement block structures, in small-town typical red brick buildings, and in large, beautiful houses of worship with stained-glass windows. I not only have had the church in my house, as scripture says, but my house has literally been in the church when, as a child, my family actually used a part of the church building as our home. My journey of faith has certainly included houses of worship.

But that is only a part of the story. A bigger part is the people who set the stage for me and those who nurtured me along the way. Grandmother King and two of her friends started Sunday school in their homes in a little town in Ohio when my mother was only a young girl. Grandmother and Granddad Benson *heard the truth,* as she relates it, as young newlyweds. It so affected their lives that later they moved ninety miles across the state of Mississippi in a wagon with my dad and his baby sister just to be close to the heart of the church in that state. She told us they were like Abraham. The Lord said to *"go to the land I will show you."*

Mother and Dad picked up the torch and lived the gospel before their young family, finally answering the call to full-time ministry when I was very young. In a new church plant, which my father started, I was given the task of playing the piano as a young teen. On the last night of a revival I faithfully completed my task of playing the final hymn—*"Only Trust Him,"* I recall. I arose from my seat at the piano and knelt at the altar of the little church and prayed a simple prayer. I told the Lord that from that moment on I was His and I would trust Him to be faithful to keep me, regardless of my doubts. And He has. Fifty years later I am more aware than ever of the importance of that decision. Since that time the journey has

Zion Lutheran Church (1856) - Marshall, Michigan

*The congregation of Zion Lutheran Church was organized
in 1856. In 1897, Rev. Christopher Heidenreich was
installed as pastor. He advocated the construction of a
building which was dedicated on December 8, 1901. The
edifice is built of solid brick and stone masonry in the
Gothic Revival architectural style. In 1937, the basement
was excavated for social gatherings and Sunday school
rooms. In 1946, Pastor Heidenreich completed fifty years of
ministry at Zion Church. His daughter at age eighty-nine
still attends services every Sunday.*

Laura Withrow

been challenging, exciting, fascinating, surprising, and rewarding, but also discouraging, difficult, and excruciatingly painful, at times. The Lord has led me into places I could never have dreamed possible and given me opportunities I could never have imagined. In the midst of it all, He has never wavered in His faithfulness to sustain and keep me as His child.

The crowning touch of this splendid life of faith is that I have had the privilege of living in partnership with a gifted and committed Christian husband. We both owe great debts of gratitude to all of the people who passed the faith on to us. The church buildings we worshipped in were important, but the people made the difference. We will never forget.

"I have been crucified with Christ and I no longer live, but Christ lives in me. The life I live in the body, I live by faith in the Son of God, who loved me and gave himself for me."
—Galatians 2:20

Into the Wider Stream

Barry L. Callen

My spiritual journey has taken an unexpected road. I was reared in a wonderful congregation in Newton Falls, Ohio, where the pastoral leadership was exceptional. The spiritual nurture was so rich that more than fifty young people from that one small-town church entered full-time Christian ministry in the congregation's first fifty years. I am one of them and have expressed my gratitude by writing the biography of the senior pastor, Reverend Lillie S. McCutcheon *(She Came Preaching, 1992)*. One theme I heard stressed on occasion was the church as God intended it, sometimes highlighted by using the failures from the long history of the Roman Catholic Church as a sad reminder of what can go wrong.

From my home church I absorbed the love of good pastoral leadership, an appreciation for nurturing young leaders, and a vision of the church as much more than any flawed human institution. After some years of my own ministry, however, my own spiritual need led me–of all places–to a Roman Catholic monastery! I became an annual Protestant retreatant in a bastion of historic Roman Catholicism. The location was the longtime home of Thomas Merton, probably the most widely published and read Roman Catholic spiritual writer of all time. The Abbey of Gethsemani has sat quietly in the hills of rural Kentucky since 1848. My visits started in the 1980s. This spiritual oasis carries on a ministry of hospitality, providing without cost spiritual retreats characterized by solitude, silence, and Christian reflection. Making the Abbey a spiritual home away from home was quite a turn from my free-church Protestant upbringing; in another way, it was

Abbey of Gethsemani (1848)
Trappist (near Bardstown), Kentucky

Abbey of Gethsemani is a monastery of Trappist monks and nuns.
Trappists believe that God calls and they are to respond by truly seeking
Him as they follow Christ in humility and obedience. With hearts
cleansed by the Word of God, by vigils, by fasting and by unceasing
conversion of life, they aim to become ever more disposed to receive from
the Holy Spirit the gift of pure and continual prayer. This search for
God is the goal of the monastic day composed of the opus Dei, lectio
divina and manual work.

The community of Trappists in Melleray, France, was flourishing so
greatly that a foundation was necessary and a friendship with the aged
Bishop Flaget drew them to Kentucky. On December 21, 1848, forty-
five founders from Melleray in western France, settled at Gethsemani.

a growing up into the wider church without denying anything precious from my youth. My pastor and church heritage had called for an elimination of denominational walls. I had begun practicing this call.

Churches can be awash in talk and activity. Ministers easily become task oriented to the point of spiritual impoverishment right in the midst of teaching and preaching about spiritual things. A capitalist society breeds surface relationships, values constant activity and acquisition, and disdains the old in favor of the every year model–that, of course, requires a new purchase or upgrade. By the 1980s I had earned my academic degrees, gathered my professional titles, traveled the world, become the hurried and honored producer of classes, committees, reports, articles, and books. The time had come for a turn. I needed balance, roots, quiet, wholeness, and wisdom.

The monastery environment, contrary to common misperception, is not intended to disdain the world. The point is an intentional holding still, being in touch with oneself and God, cherishing the long tradition of God in the world, actually practicing prayer and God's presence, relishing the sweet sounds of silence, and finally realizing that true value lies first in *being* rather than in *doing*. My book *Authentic Spirituality (Baker Books, 2002)* highlights the several streams of Christian spirituality, including the contemplative. Does this make me a Protestant or Catholic? The answer is, I now am a Christian who belongs to the whole church, protests on occasion, and chooses to be *catholic* in the best sense. I am reaching for the wider stream of Christian riches. This journey of renewal has only begun for me, but at least the corner has been turned!

"During the fourth watch of the night Jesus went out to them, walking on the lake. When the disciples saw him walking on the lake, they were terrified. 'It's a ghost,' they said, and cried out in fear. But Jesus immediately said to them: 'Take courage! It is I. Don't be afraid.'"

—Matthew 14:25-27

When Doubts Fade Away

Leonard W. Snyder

Though the experiences of others can be great lessons for us, there are some things that must be experienced personally if we are to appreciate them fully. Who, with a thousand words, could ever help you enjoy the taste of a dish of chocolate ice cream? Or who, with countless pictures or hours of video, could ever help you experience the joy of holding your son or daughter for the first time?

It was that way with me on our first trip to Israel. I said little about my two growing concerns to the small group of people who had committed to join us. The first concern was for our personal security. Because several people had just been killed in Hebron, I thought of canceling the trip. The second one was too personal to mention, so strange that I hardly wanted to deal with it myself. "What if I go there and visit the places and see the sights and then find I don't believe it happened like I have been reading and preaching? What would I do then?"

I suppose the personal security threat never completely went away. There was the presence of the military and the scars on the buildings left by gun shots in recent local battles. All of this served to remind me that the Holy Land was not a place where the way of holiness had always been evident.

My second concern began to fade when we were riding on the bus and I saw, for the first time, road signs to places like Nazareth, Jericho, Jerusalem, Bethlehem. My heart began to pound as names from the Bible became actual destinations for our trip. As we rode along, the Arab Christian guide explained the historical significance of passing scenes and of the place we were to visit next. When we walked

St. Peter's Catholic Church (1851) - *Charlotte, North Carolina*

Rev. Jeremiah O'Connell, a circuit riding priest based in Columbia, South Carolina spent two days on a stagecoach to travel to Charlotte and lay the cornerstone for the first St. Peter's Church on March 25, 1851. The cost for two areas of land and St. Peter's Church was $1,000. Much of the money was given by non-Catholics who liked Father Jeremiah when he preached at the Episcopal Church.

In 1892, members of the Benedictine Order from Belmont Abbey began their service to St. Peter's. A gentle spirit, Father Francis Meyer, came to be pastor and the present church was built a short time later. In 1960, the Diocesan priests began serving the church. Since its rebirth in 1986 when Jesuits came to serve, the parish has grown to 750 families. The congregation has a strong commitment to the poor and to the civic life of the community.

around each area, the *ohs* and *ahs* only partially expressed our awe at what we were feeling and seeing. Nothing new, for millions of people over hundreds of years had seen the same things. The difference was the fact that they were new sights and experiences for us.

Finally, we came to the Sea of Galilee. Some might say it was just a good-sized fishing lake with mountains on each side, but for me it suddenly erased the final shred of doubt. This was the place! Not just a blue spot on a map in the back of my Bible nor the mentioned location in some Bible verse, but the actual lake where our Lord walked on the water and around which much of His ministry took place. Why had I ever wondered or even doubted? This was the place, and the faith that had brought my life under the Lordship of Christ many years before was immediately strengthened by what I was seeing and experiencing.

One trip there was not enough to satisfy my desire to know more about the "place where Jesus walked." And one reading of the Bible is not enough to satisfy my desire to know the God of the Book and to discover all the road signs that are there for my life. He *is* real and He *is* really *my* Lord!

"God, whom I serve with my whole heart in preaching the gospel of his Son, is my witness how constantly I remember you in my prayers at all times; and I pray that now at last by God's will the way may be opened for me to come to you."
—Romans 1:9-10

My Journey Times Three

Geraldine Hurst Reardon

I was a child–
I remember the lilac bush by the old well,
The white and pink peonies that bloom
each year by Memorial Day.
The shaded bench under the grape arbour,
The cherry tree, and the raspberry
bushes which yielded
to our stained fingers purple fruit
for breakfast.

I remember playing house,
playing store, playing church:
And I recall building a sand
throne and ornamenting it
with a rainbow of petunias.

I remember the stairway that led to
grandmother's room with its
featherbed.
The firelight's dancing shadows as I drifted
off to sleep,
Mother's piano-playing, mother's
praying in the moonlight,
Mother's dying at age thirty-three!

I am a mother–
I've shared with God and my
beloved the miracle of creation.
I've cradled within my body a new, little person.

Geraldine Reardon
1917-2001

157

West Side Conservative Baptist Church
Block Island, Rhode Island

I remember the pain, the pushing, the breaking, the rending,
And four times the magic words, "You have a healthy baby."
I remember the nursing, the rocking, the bathing,
First tooth, first step, first word;
Little books, little songs, little prayers;
Recitals, madrigals, school plays;
First dates, first loves, first heartbreaks;
Trips to the mountains, the ocean, overseas.

I remember the wrenching in the heart at separation
The empty places at the table,
the quiet rooms heavy with memories.
The deep ache in the heart when children, finding themselves
and freedom, are hurt and disillusioned.
But the loving, the sharing, the playing, the singing,
the listening, the worshipping are always there.

I will be a grandmother—
And now my little girl is to become a mother!
The doctor has heard the heartbeat:
She has felt the flutter and kick of life.
The family life force goes on—the family tree is growing!
What will the little one look like?
What family traits will he or she show?
How will it feel to hold my grandchild and
see him smile with unfocused eyes at me?
What emotion will I experience when
I see my daughter nursing her baby in Madonna-like repose?
When October turns the leaves to gold, I will begin to know.

"...Sing and make music in your heart to the Lord, always giving thanks to God the Father for everything, in the name of our Lord Jesus Christ."
—Ephesians 5:19-20

Harmonizing in a Little Country Church

Dale D. Landis

*J*erry, Bill, Jack and I had just set up the sound system and had a short rehearsal with Jeannine, our pianist, in the open-air tabernacle in southeast Indiana. The pew benches were old and rickety, the floor was dirt and gravel, the old piano on the stage was out of tune and seemed to have more spider webs than strings in it. We were sitting in the little lunchroom eating a sandwich and my mind's eye was traveling from the trees outside the window to some other trees I remembered fifty years earlier in southern Ohio.

Dad had driven our family, in our old gray 1948 Chevy, to the hills close to the Ohio River. We wandered off the highway, through some windy, country roads until we saw the little church, painted white and sitting up on the hill beyond the trees. My uncles, Harry, Henry and Clarence and their families were following us. They were the guest quartet who was to sing at the church that day. There were cars parked among the trees in the woods and all around the church.

We walked up the hill toward the church and we could hear singing coming from the open windows. It was spring, and everything around us, including the little church, just seemed to be a part of God's creation. There were wooden steps leading up to the door in the front, and as I walked up them, I looked high above me and the little white steeple seemed to be leaning into the fluffy clouds floating by. Some very wonderful people who looked just like the people from my church back home greeted us.

We all found a seat in the hard wooden pews, and I noticed that the smiles and excitement of the people crowded into the room, warmed the cold, plain walls and the simple lights hanging from the ceiling. The only carpet in the room was on a small platform up in

The Apostolic Church of Jesus Christ
Brown County, Indiana

the front. Behind the old pine pulpit was a picture of the Jordan River, painted on the wall. A preacher came to the front of the church and welcomed everyone to the service. We sang a hymn and Dad's quartet was introduced.

They walked to the front, stood close together on the small platform, and Uncle Harry, the bass, took a pitch pipe out of his coat pocket and blew a note. They all hummed a chord and began singing hymns and songs about Jesus, salvation, and heaven. I sat close to mom and didn't want the singing to ever end. Well, it did, and the preacher came up to the front again, thanked Dad and the uncles, and invited everyone outside for a dinner on the grounds.

What a surprise I saw when we went out onto the lawn. Someone had set up long boards on sawhorses, placed tablecloths on them and they were covered with the most wonderful food I had ever seen. Fried chicken, roast beef, homemade noodles, mashed potatoes, green beans, corn, fresh bread, and of course, pies and cakes. One table had big crocks of lemonade.

Everyone ate and enjoyed talking and visiting with everyone else. Even though Dad and the uncles had never met these people, they all seemed to know each other and shared a common *thing*. We sat on car bumpers, logs, make-shift benches and the grass. After everyone was done eating, Dad and the uncles sang some more songs out under the trees.

That little church, those gospel quartet songs, and the wonderful love of those brothers and sisters never moved out of my six-year-old heart. Our families finally loaded back into our cars and headed home. I went to more sings and never lost my love for gospel quartet music. It was some years later, when my voice was changing, that one night at quartet practice around the piano in our living room, Dad asked me if I would like to harmonize with them. They were singing *Just a Little Talk with Jesus*. They had sung that song at the little, white-painted church. I stood next to Dad and sang out the tenor part with him as loud as I could.

Back at the campgrounds in southern Indiana, with microphones, speakers, and tape decks, our quartet is singing *Just a Little Talk with Jesus*. And my mind floats back from that little church in the hilly woods, and I thank God for that wonderful moment when He revealed Himself to me in such a wonderful, mystical way.

"...there is now no condemnation to those who are in Christ Jesus, because through
Christ Jesus the law of the Spirit of life set me free from the law of sin and death.
–Romans 8:1-2

A Heritage of Faith

Frederick G. Shackleton

That May morning dawned as pretty as one could imagine. Situated among great old trees on the gentle slope of a hillside, our house was an ideal spot from which to view the morning, especially from my upstairs bedroom window. But my stomach suggested that it was time for breakfast. I hurried down the stairs.

As I entered the family room, I discovered that something was terribly wrong. Our pastor and a friend had joined my mother and older brothers around a cot where my father lay crying out in pain. As best a ten-year-old could, I began to piece together the situation.

At daybreak my father had gone out to tend to a cow that had gotten loose. But he was suddenly in such pain that he had to come inside. Our pastor was called to pray for him.

Frederick G. Shackleton

It was a Monday morning. I recalled the testimony my father had given at the church service the night before. He had quoted Romans 8:1, *"There is therefore now no condemnation to them which are in Christ Jesus, who walk not after the flesh, but after the Spirit."* His concluding

St. Ann's Episcopal Church (1893)
Kennebunkport, Maine

*St. Ann's Church offically organized in 1883 and construction
on the building was begun in August, 1887, and was
dedicated on August 24, 1893. It is listed on the National
Register of Historic Places. Henry Paston Clark of Boston was
the architect.*

*Former President George Bush and Barbara Bush consider
this their home church during the summer months.*

words were *"I have no condemnation."* Now he still had no condemnation, but he had a great deal of pain. It seemed to center in his lower abdomen, creating fierce spasms that doubled him up.

A doctor was called. After the doctor ran his fingers over Father's swollen abdomen, he said, "We'll have to take you to the hospital." My father said, in his agonized voice, "Oh doctor, I can't go to the hospital. I have no money and no insurance." This was in the midst of the Great Depression.

But the doctor said, "We can't let you just lie here and suffer. I'll make the arrangements." He got in his car and left. My oldest brother picked Father up, put him in his Model A Ford, and drove to the hospital.

The hospital treatments made Father a bit more comfortable and later that day we were able to visit him. He had some personal words for each of us. We learned that he was to have surgery the next day.

During the surgery, a messenger came to the waiting room and told us the surgeon wanted us to come to the operating room, a highly unusual procedure. We stood near the doorway. We saw Father on the operating table. The surgeon lifted out a length of intestine which was swollen, blackened and inflamed, which he said he would have to remove. We gathered that Father's chance of survival was small and the doctor wanted us to understand why. This was before the day of antibiotics.

Father died early the next morning. Mother had spent the night in his room. When the rest of us entered, she put her arm around me and said "Papa's gone."

We went through the next few months mechanically, doing what had to be done, shaken by a great grief, but buoyed up and comforted by remembering his last testimony, "I have no condemnation."

My father was a farmer, a devoted father and a devout Christian. He would have liked to have had the education to follow the tug in his heart to preach. Three of his sons became ordained ministers in the Church of God. The fourth was a loyal churchman.

As I write this, nearly seven decades later, I am thankful for the heritage of faith which is mine—a faith that sustained us through this crisis and other testing times to come.

"Your love, O LORD, reaches to the heavens,
your faithfulness to the skies."
—Psalm 36:5

Retracing Steps

Judy Craig Bradley

My childhood was spent on Church Street in a small town in Virginia. I was not aware that the street even had a name, but I was aware that the church our family attended was on this street. And the church was the center of the life of my family and my life as a child.

Recently, my husband went with me to retrace the steps of my childhood. A flood of memories surfaced as I stood on the ground where the house I was born in once stood. In this house, family from across southwest Virginia would gather after church on Sunday for some of my mother's very best fried chicken and other southern delicacies. I got to eat last, but I enjoyed the laughter and sensed the love in the stories that I heard.

Members of my family contributed greatly in my development as a Christian. Prayer was an important part of our lives. Many times in my childhood and teen years I heard prayers to God asking for the provision of material and spiritual needs. Prayer for everything was a way of life. My mother would often give our tithe and then pray that we would have the necessities of life. Though we did not have much, we always received what we needed.

The church building stands next door to where I lived as a child. The entire family, all of my dad's brothers and sisters, attended this congregation. More special memories came to me as I entered this building for the first time in many years. In this special place I learned the hymns of the church and heard several pastors preach God's wonderful message of love. The church became my life early in my life. Since I had learned to play the piano at an early age, by the time I was twelve years old I was playing in the worship services.

Often, while practicing on the piano in the church, I would talk with God about my dreams of leading choirs and teaching children in the church. God and I had many conversations in this small church building concerning my future. I learned to have a confident faith in God. I had seen in my mother's faith and the faith of other

First Church of God (1932) - *Rich Creek, Virginia*

The congregation in Rich Creek was begun in 1932 by some interested persons who had received the message of the Church of God. Mrs. Gertrude Craig Rice started a Sunday school.

Among the early pastoral leaders were persons such as Rev. Boyd Williams and Rev. Lewis Thomas. The congregation is "on a hill" in a small town and continues its ministry after almost three quarters of a century.

family members that God honors our faith.

The church, God's people and family surrounded me with love throughout my early years. And it was in this same community that our wedding was conducted. We have been married for forty-one years. As I stood once again in this house of worship, I remembered the pastor who performed our ceremony. He was supportive and exuded a confidence that God would take care of us and guide us through the future. How could I have ever known that he was a representative of many stalwarts of faith that God would bring into my life? As we walked through the cemetery as a part of this *retracing of steps,* I saw the names of my family members whose faith I would remember and see reflected in the lives of numerous others during my life. Thank you families of faith!

Worship has continued to be an important component of my life. As we worshipped in the church of my childhood, there were few persons that I knew. However, the Spirit of God was the same and loving hands of caring people continue to maintain the facility. The people and pastor worship our loving God. It has been my joy to worship and be a part of the church on several continents. These places are a long way from Church Street in the mountains of Virginia. How thankful I am that God's people have been so gracious, loving and supportive throughout my life.

My journey with my husband has taken us to four pastorates, where we met so many dynamic persons of faith. These servants of God have left many positive images on my heart. Then I met many more persons of faith, leaders, administrators and international brothers and sisters when I worked in the national offices. How many times my husband would look at me and say, "This is a long way from Church Street." This was not to demean the place that nurtured me, but to honor God as our journey was blessed so very much with so many.

From the Saturday evening *song fests* with family to a little building in Germany where people heard the hymns and songs of faith in public for the first time in many years, God has been good. My prayer now is one of thanksgiving. Thank you to the congregation in Rich Creek and thank you to all the saints of the Church of God for having faith in me. Thank you, church, for your faith. Now I pray that our children will have seen the faith of parents and will share it with their families. God is so good. "My faith looks up to thee…"

"...I do not consider myself yet to have taken hold of it. But one thing I do: Forgetting what is behind and straining toward what is ahead, I press on toward the goal to win the prize for which God has called me heavenward in Christ Jesus."
—Philippians 3:13-14

God's Guidance Amidst Life's Changes

David L. Coolidge

After forty-two years of serving as a busy pastor, in a variety of assignments in youth ministry, music ministry, worship leadership, visitation, and pastoral care, I decided to retire from full-time ministry two years ago. This was not a quick or easy decision; I had spent months thinking and praying about it. Adjustment to retirement, especially in the first few months, was difficult for me. There were times when I greatly missed former pastoral duties and responsibilities and other moments when I felt I was only an observer on the sidelines of the playing field of life. I longed for a renewed sense of purpose in my life and a new focus in my vocation as a minister.

Trusting God for guidance seems easier when things are predictable and comfortable; but when major changes come or problems arise, one's faith can be challenged. A turning point in my life occurred at the time of the month-long illness and unanticipated passing of a close personal friend and ministerial colleague, Anita Smith Womack. During the weeks of her long hospitalization in St. Vincent Hospital's ICU in the spring of 2000 and my many hospital visits to be with her and her husband, Joe, I felt the need to send frequent email reports and updates on her state of health to her many friends at home and abroad who had access to email. Having been on the worldwide web for only a little more than a year at that time, the number of email screen name additions to my address book had been increasing. In response to my widespread emails, many persons began to express their appreciation for my emails to them. Many others soon asked to be added to my mailing list. In the nineteen months since Anita's untimely passing, I have felt led to

New Park Place Church of God (1906) - Anderson, Indiana

In 1945, Park Place Church had outgrown its facilities on Eighth and College. The new pastor, W. Dale Oldham looked toward expanding the old church site. Eventually the church bought lots that were traded for the old Park Place School site. The new building was erected at East Fifth and College Drive. The church's 150-foot tower would rise as a witness to the east side of Anderson and across the river to the downtown area.

On Sunday, May 29, 1960, Dr. Oldham, carrying the pulpit Bible, led the procession up the hill to the new edifice. He was followed by other ministers, leaders, and the congregation. The old church building was given as a gift to Anderson College.

continue sending frequent emails about notable happenings (births, weddings, anniversaries, achievements, awards and recognitions, special events and occasions, serious illnesses, major surgeries, accidents, deaths, concerns, etc.) in the lives of persons in or related to our church, university and local communities. Frequently, people have asked me to pass along prayer requests to persons on my extensive emailing list.

Thus, I believe that God has led me into a new role of service in pastoral care–what many friends refer to as *my email ministry*. I thank God for the privilege of utilizing the wonderful tool of email that makes possible such rapid communication with persons around the world! As each new day dawns, I am discovering new opportunities to continue in ministry. I am now enjoying life fully as a retiree and have confidence in God's leading in my life. It is reassuring to know that God has guided me in the past, is with me in the present, and will be with me in all my unknown tomorrows.

Anita Smith Womack
1937-2000

"You are all sons of God through faith in Christ Jesus, for all of you who were baptized into Christ have clothed yourselves with Christ. There is neither Jew nor Greek, slave nor free, male nor female, for you are all one in Christ Jesus. If you belong to Christ, then you are Abraham's seed, and heirs according to the promise."
–Galatians 3:26-29

From Tragedy to Faith

Philip L. Kinley

My childhood in the 1930s was not as primitive as Laura Wilder's *Little House on the Prairie*, but there were common experiences. Living in rural Kansas we had no electricity, running water, or modern conveniences taken for granted today. This simple lifestyle had an impact on me and my family's accepting Christ as our Lord and Savior.

At our house, Mother did laundry on a washboard and heated flat-irons on the kerosene kitchen stove. One cold spring day Mother spent the day ironing. Father was away at work and my brother and I were at school. Only Mother and my five-year-old sister were at home. By early afternoon fuel for the heating stove was low. Mother went to gather wood and coal, urging my sister to remain inside where it was warm. She became anxious and pulled a chair to the kitchen window to find her mother. As she climbed onto the chair, she fell against the stove with the high flames heating the flat-irons. Her clothing caught fire and she was severely burned. After lingering in the hospital for a week she died. This was a tremendous shock to our family, especially Dad and Mom. Until this time, Dad was not interested in God, neither did he wish to know Him or anything spiritual. The death of his daughter left him with an unfathomable emotional void and he began to question the meaning of life and one's relationship to God.

The following summer after my sister's death, students from a nearby Bible college came to our little community church to conduct Vacation Bible School for children and evening evangelistic services for the public.

Tamagawa Church of God (1953) - *Tokyo, Japan*

The Tamagawa Church of God was started in 1953 by missionaries Arthur and Norma Eikamp. It is located near the Church of God Junior-Senior High School, Tamagawa Seigakuin. It ministers to both students and the surrounding community.

We children had attended Sunday School with our mother from the time of my earliest memories, but always without my father. As a result of the weeks of wrestling with himself over matters concerning life and death, he decided to attend evangelistic services with the family.

Each evening the students took turns explaining the meaning of salvation and trust in God. As a nine-year-old, I sat on the front row of our little church and tried to absorb what I heard. Although I did not understand much of what was spoken, I felt a deep longing to know God. At the last service of the two-week series, an invitation was given to accept Jesus Christ as Savior. All who would believe were encouraged to raise their hands. I knew I wanted to believe so I raised my hand. At the conclusion of the service, the evangelist encouraged those who raised hands to procede to a small room at the back of the sanctuary for further counseling. As I entered this room I was very surprised to see my father. It was then I realized he had made his faith commitment at the same time as I had. My decision has had a double blessing for me. First, even though a child, I became a child of God through faith. Second, the fact that Dad and I were born into the Kingdom the same night has been an encouragement to me in my faith journey. Through the experience of an adult as a newborn Christian, he was able to assist me as a child to persist and grow in my faith.

Today, I look back over Dad's fifty-five-year journey of faith, and marvel at the power of God to make him into a new creation who loved the Lord until death. I am deeply grateful for His grace to a nine-year-old who wanted to know God. I also marvel that He could work through a tragedy in our home *"...for the good of those who love him, who have been called according to his purpose."*
–Romans 8:28

"When he arrived and saw the evidence of the grace of God, he was glad and encouraged them all to remain true to the Lord with all their hearts. He was a good man, full of the Holy Spirit and faith..."
—Acts 11:23-24

A Man of Faith and Good Works

Phyllis Gillespie Kinley

In the late 1940s, my brother Gwain, assigned to write an article about our father, told the story of Diogenes (412-323 B.C.), a Greek philosopher, who went through the streets of Athens carrying a lighted lantern, looking for an honest man. "My father is that honest man," he wrote. "He is also a man of faith."

In the waning years of the Great Depression, Dad gave up a successful business to move to Owatonna in southern Minnesota so that his children could experience life within a thriving Church of God congregation. We were loved, inspired, and nurtured by a succession of wonderful pastors and their wives.

Dad found the answer to life and faith in James 4:15 *"...if it is the Lord's will, we will live and do this or that."* When oil wells began to appear around our small portion of family land in West Virginia and we waited to learn if oil would be found there, my father cautioned us, "the Lord willing." But nothing was left to us. Large oil companies working on surrounding farms drew out the oil from beneath our land. We learned to depend on hard work and God's faithfulness rather than material wealth. During the following years when life brought other kinds of loss, we found strength in acceptance and trust, in the security of a Father's love, and in a growing partnership with God in every area of life.

The summer of 1947, just before my senior year in high school, I broke into tears while weeding with my mother in the cornfield. "You know we don't have any money for college, Mom," I said, tears falling on the hot rich soil at my feet. "I'm afraid I won't be able to go to Anderson College next year."

When my mother spoke, I remembered again my father's "the

Hagiyama Church of God (1975) - *Tokyo, Japan*

Hagiyama church had its beginnings in 1975 under the leadership of missionaries Philip and Phyllis Kinley. The congregation worshiped in the Seminary House facilities until the present structure was completed in 1996.

Lord willing." "God has a plan for you," she said firmly. "Let's trust Him to work out the details."

One morning that fall, the principal of my high school called me to his office. I learned I had been chosen by the faculty to receive a scholarship to any college or university in the United States. I would meet often with a lawyer during those four years to express thanks, but I would never know either the donor's name or face. However, I learned that the generosity taught me by that unknown donor, and the faith mentored by my mother and father gave me an anchor when life dealt some blows later in our years in Japan.

God used his own timing and methods to give us children when we could not have some of our own. Physically and financially we could not return to America to care for our son, Tom, when he was hit by a car in Chicago, or when our daughter, Susan, was in an accident in Indiana. God used other persons to care for them instead.

In 1992, my father called me from his nursing home in Owatonna. His cancer had returned and he was in pain. "You pray that I will die," he said.

"Dad, you've always said 'the Lord willing.'"

"Yes, I know," he broke in, "but I want to go now." I prayed. Two weeks later, my alert ninety-nine and a half- year-old father, after spending one day in bed, died not of cancer, but of pneumonia.

Dad was faithful. And once again, the Lord was both faithful and "willing."

Philip and Phyllis Kinley

*"Therefore, as we have opportunity, let us do good to all people,
especially to those who belong to the family of believers."*
—Galatians 6:10

The Beginning

James L. Sparks

Among Anderson University's splendid programs is Tri-S, Student Summer Service. In the summer of 1968, I had the opportunity to serve as a pastor to a small congregation in a small town. The church needed a summer pastor until their newly-called pastor would arrive in the fall. I was chosen to serve with fellow ministerial student Ken Ray. Together we agreed on financial arrangements and transportation, and within days we were pulling into Palmyra, the birthplace of Joseph Smith, a sleepy village of 1,000 near the Finger Lakes in upstate New York.

The church on the main north-south street of town was painted white with mahogany trim. The interior had the same mahogany wood on the pulpit and chancel furniture with white trim on the pews. The rectangular sanctuary had a mirror image fellowship hall in the basement that had curtains dividing it into classrooms. It was a small building, on a small lot, in a small village well off the New York Throughway. To Ken and me, however, it was very special.

Dividing the work evenly, Ken would preach in the morning service, and I would bring the evening message, reversing the order the next Sunday. We collaborated on what to inscribe in the Bibles given to high school graduates, which homes to visit, what curriculum lessons to teach, even what dinner invitations to accept. Because there was only one office in the corner of the basement, we constructed a makeshift desk in one of the classrooms. One of my fondest memories is of working on a lesson or a sermon while listening to Ken praying just around the corner. It was the ideal beginning for a lifetime of team ministry.

Since that time, I have served in a variety of settings, from modest to grand, in congregations varying in size from sixty to sixteen hundred, from doctors and lawyers to coalminers and cereal workers, but I've never forgotten the place where ministry began for me, where I took the first tentative, wobbling steps of servanthood, where I learned the value of working in a yoke. That beginning has made such a difference.

Whitetop Baptist Church (1901)
Whitetop, Virginia

"Then he said to his disciples, 'the harvest is plentiful but the workers are few. Ask the Lord of the harvest, therefore, to send out workers into his harvest field.'"
—Matthew 9:37-38

An Important Decision in My Faith Journey

Nathan L. Smith

For five years after I started thinking and praying about my future life's work, I did not receive a clear sense of direction except that I should study and prepare myself for Christian service.

While serving as a member of the U.S. military occupation forces in Japan in the fall of 1945, I had the opportunity of helping some women missionaries who had managed to stay in Japan during World War II. My contact with them had a profound influence on my life. Their vision for the evangelization of Japan became my vision.

I knew that country was wide open to the gospel. My prayer became "Lord, send missionaries to sow the seed and reap the harvest."

Finally I seemed to hear Him asking, "Nathan, what are you going to do about it?" As that question tugged at my heart I replied, "Lord, if you can use this poor farmboy, here I am." From that moment I found peace. My goal became clear to prepare and get back to Japan as soon as possible.

As a result of that experience I had the joyful privilege of serving as a missionary in Asia for thirty years; twenty-six years in Japan and four in South Korea.

Tachikawa Church of God (1952) - *Tokyo, Japan*

The Tachikawa Church of God was begun in 1952 under the leadership of missionaries Nathan and Ann Smith. The nucleus for the congregation came from a Bible study group for Japanese workers at the Tachikawa Airbase.

"Let me live that I may praise you, and may your laws sustain me."
—Psalm 119:175

The Lord Is with Me...

Ilene Gray Bargerstock

itting on the edge of the narrow examining table in the doctor's office, legs dangling, too short to reach the foot rest, lower body covered by a thin paper sheet, I was anxious to learn why the nurse had called me at work that morning to say the doctor wanted to see me. After all, I was feeling fine again. She said, "You might want to bring your husband."

I'd been admitted to the hospital a few weeks earlier with severe stomach pain. I was told my body was reacting as some do who have been on prolonged antibiotics. I had not taken any such medication. Numerous tests did not reveal the problem. The doctor spoke of possible exploratory surgery and called colleagues in other cities for advice. Then the symptoms stopped. Before releasing me, the doctor scheduled an appointment at his office in a couple of weeks. At that time, he examined me and I reported how good I was feeling. He said he wanted to order one more test–one that I was too ill to tolerate while in the hospital. I'd had the test and now here I was.

After the usual pleasantries, the doctor held a sheet of paper in front of me, and it became increasingly difficult to focus while, in soft tones, he explained the digestive tract and concluded by placing an "X" in the spot where "it" was. "It" being the tumor that he felt most certain was cancerous. The surgery was scheduled. I must have said something or asked some questions, but I don't even remember getting dressed and leaving.

That was a life-defining moment for me. One of those times when you must step out of your secure lifeboat into the murky waters of uncertainty and see if the faith you have long professed will hold you up and carry you through whatever is to come. It was scary.

It is clear that God was with me all the way, just as I always said I believed He would be. I've never believed that, in a time of trouble, I could just open the Bible at random and put my finger on

Jersey Shore Church of God (1926) - *Jersey Shore, Pennsylvania*

The Church of God in Jersey Shore was the outgrowth of the efforts of Mr. and Mrs. George Ramer. Through Bible studies and the distribution of the Gospel Trumpet, Mr. Ramer aroused many people to the fellowship of the church. Services were held for several years in the Ramer home. The church building was purchased in November, 1926, from the Presbyterian Church.

a scripture that would be helpful. However, at that time, I happened to be following one of those prescribed plans for reading the Bible through in one year and was in the book of Psalms. The day the doctor gave me the news, the assigned reading was chapter 118. Verse 6 said, *"The LORD is with me; I will not be afraid;"* verse 14, *"The LORD is my strength and my song;"* and verse 17, *"I will not die but live, and will proclaim what the LORD has done."*

During the thirteen days between the diagnosis and the surgery, every day's reading seemed to have something just for me–Psalm 119, verse 50, *"My comfort in my suffering is this: Your promise preserves my life;"* verses 145-149, *"I call with all my heart; answer me, O LORD, ...I rise before dawn and cry for help; I have put my hope in your word. My eyes stay open through the watches of the night, that I may meditate on your promises. Hear my voice in accordance with your love; preserve my life, O LORD, according to your laws,"* and verse 175, *"Let me live that I may praise you..."*

One of my greatest concerns was the possibility of not sharing in the lives of my grandchildren, two of whom were just babies. The day after the surgery, when the report came back that the lymph nodes were clear and it was believed that all the cancer cells had been removed and no chemo required, the reading assignment was Psalm 128 which proclaims in verses 5 and 6, *"May the LORD bless you from Zion all the days of your life; may you see the prosperity of Jerusalem, and may you live to see your children's children. Peace be upon 'Israel'"* (Here I inserted my own name).

That was nine years ago and I had eight grandchildren. Now I have ten, and I thank God for them everyday.

Also, I thank God for the doctor whose God-given instincts would not allow him to dismiss me just because I was feeling good. He could find no medical or logical link between the mysterious symptoms that drove me to the hospital and what was discovered in that final test. The location of the tumor was such that it is called the *silent killer,* because it often goes undetected and without symptoms until it is out of control.

One last scripture–this the day I went home from the hospital, *"I will not enter my house or go to my bed–I will allow no sleep to my eyes, no slumber to my eyelids, till I find a place for the LORD, a dwelling place for the Mighty One..."* –Psalm 132:3-5. That dwelling place, of course, is within my forever grateful heart.

"O LORD, hear my prayer, listen to my cry for mercy;
in your faithfulness and righteousness come to my relief."
—Psalm 143:1

Faith:
An Absolute Necessity

Fredrick H. Shively

I learned that life's greatest lessons, especially as related to faith, come through the difficult times. I was in my third year as pastor of the Inter-Community Church of God in Covina, California. The ministry was going well and life was very good. Kay and I had a son, Kevin, who was nearing two years of age. Kay was very near the delivery of our second child, who turned out to be Mark.

I had played racquetball with a friend and had not done particularly well, but that was not so unusual. I soon realized, however, that I was not feeling well. A visit to the doctor showed a high white blood cell count and I was ordered to rest. The same physician called two days later to state that he wanted to see me again. Kay, who had talked to him, relayed the news to me. She was not going to tell me exactly what the doctor said, but her face betrayed her true feelings. I insisted that she tell me. The doctor suspected something much more serious than the original diagnosis; we inferred leukemia, though he did not use the word.

After receiving that news we began a five-day odyssey of faith. I had to wait from Thursday to the following Tuesday for the test results. My mind raced. I was thirty, at the beginning of a ministry. We had one son and awaited another. I wanted very much to see them grow up. I wanted very much to live a long life. And yet, I knew that not everyone has that opportunity.

Of course I prayed. In the middle of my prayers, I had many different emotions. I do not remember bargaining with God, but I earnestly prayed for God's presence. I am not a person who likes to listen to television preachers. Most of them seem far more interested in their own power and well-being than in announcing truly good

Inter-Community Church of God (1962) - Covina, California

In May of 1967, Fred Shively was called to the Inter-Community Church of God in Covina, California. At that time the congregation was worshiping in the Women's Club of Covina. A new church building for this congregation was under construction. This new congregation was the result of a merger of the Church of God congregations in Baldwin Park and Glendora.

There were four building programs during the six years that Dr. Shively pastored there. The congregation grew and the building represented the commitments to ministry that exemplified them. Every stage of construction brought a new sense of excitement as the congregation itself did the work of construction.

news. However, on Sunday morning, I listened to a message that I have never forgotten. Robert Schuller, whom I knew, pastor of the large Dutch Reformed Church in Garden Grove, spoke on the subject, "Faith in God is no luxury; it is an absolute necessity." I do not remember the rest of the sermon, but this one line, as simple as it was, sustained me. I came to a point that, no matter what happened to me, I was going to trust God. I know that I faced the possibility of death, and discovered that I did not have to fear.

When the news came that I had a serious form of mononucleosis, we were overjoyed. Kay said, "I don't care how serious it is; it isn't leukemia." She then turned her attention to delivering our baby; she had refused to go forward until she knew that I was going to be okay. Mark was born shortly after that.

Although I was in bed for seven weeks with my liver and spleen swollen to twice their normal size with two-year-old Kevin wanting to jump up and down on Daddy, we managed very well.

That story happened more than half my present life ago, and yet, the lesson I learned has stayed with me. I have shared it with my family and many others: "Faith in God is no luxury; it is an absolute necessity."

"And whoever welcomes a little child like this in my name welcomes me."
—Matthew 18:5

When I'm Seven, I'll Get Saved

John L. Albright

Our family hadn't gone to church for years. We were too busy with other things. Well actually, Mom had taken me once or twice to Sunday school a few miles away; the denomination she had known as a child in Arcadia, Indiana. But that doesn't count. Trust me, we hadn't gone to church for years.

What is now sprawling suburbia south of Indianapolis was mostly wide-open farmland when I was a kid. A country block away, at a country crossroads, was the Meridian Church of God. One pastor, who had no car, occasionally walked to our house for a visit. Sometimes, when he knocked, my parents pretended not to be home.

Those were the days of two and three-week revival meetings. A preacher, advertised as a *Cowboy Evangelist,* was to come to that church. He strummed a guitar, sang and preached. Since we owned horses, and loved going to rodeos, the revival promotion caught the attention of my older brother—twelve years old at the time. He went to services several nights in a row. "You oughtta hear that guy sing!" he exclaimed to Mom and Dad.

When Dad told this story, it took a half-hour. It became a part of his testimony, when years later, he and Mom traveled as music evangelists in revivals and campmeetings. Boy, could Dad sing, and boy, could Mom play the piano and organ!

Briefly told, my brother was saved and, through a series of heart-touching events, was the means of my parents experiencing salvation, all in the same revival.

I was six years old at the time. I don't remember this conversation, but Mom told me many times that I said, "I'm not old enough to become a Christian yet, but as soon as I'm seven, then I'll get saved." And I did just that, making my way to the kneeling rail at the front of our church.

Meridian Church of God (1939)
originally called "The County Line Church of God"
Indianapolis, Indiana

In 1938, Louise Rigdon experienced a vision from God. She saw children marching in and out of her house while a young girl played the piano. The girl would stop playing and that picture would fade and a white frame building would appear. Louise had never considered herself a visionary. The Rigdons counseled with their pastor, John Williams. He encouraged them to proceed with beginning a new church. The first Sunday school class was held on October 8, 1939. There were nine children plus the Rigdon family of five.

What started as a children's class grew as adults began attending. In February, 1939, the class moved to the garage. In 1942, the congregation obtained a loan and began construction on a new building with a full basement. In 1965, the sanctuary was remodeled and a wing for office, kindergarten and nursery was added. This included an area for classrooms and a fellowship hall. A new sanctuary was built and dedicated in 1972.

Since that day, I have never felt outside of the will of a loving, accepting God. Perfect? Of course not. I searched, questioned, doubted, but I was reared to believe that God understands and affirms honest inquiry.

Thanks to encouraging and supportive pastors, my own wonderful parents, my many moms and dads in the faith, and our church's institutions of higher learning, I was nurtured to maturity and taught that my faith journey never ends, but is always open to new truth and growth in the Lord. As a pastor today, I continue to try to relate that truth to others.

What does a seven-year-old know about salvation? Not much. But at that time, I began to learn, thanks to all those wonderful, caring, loving adults who saw potential in one, little country boy.

Anita's Prayer

Thank you for the children and youth. Bless them, we pray, as they experiment, try out, create. Protect them from evil and guide them. May the choices they make, the friends they choose be in line with your will for their lives.

Give us, we pray, comfort in our questions. Remind us that a good question holds as much grace as an answer. Keep our questions alive that we may always be seekers rather that settlers. Make us, we pray, a wondering, far-sighted, questioning, restless people.

And give us the feet of pilgrims on this journey unfinished, as we walk with You and with one another in this world.

In Jesus' name,
Amen.

Anita Smith Womack, 1937-2000, former Director of the Children's Center and Minister of Christian Education, Park Place Church of God, Anderson, Indiana.

"'For I know the plans I have for you,' declares the LORD, 'plans to prosper you and not to harm you, plans to give you hope and a future.'"
—Jeremiah 29:11

Cloud on the Mountain

Cheryl Johnson Barton

The audible voice of God? I've never heard it. But I have no doubt God spoke that day through the cloud on the mountain.

It had been a difficult few years. My husband and I had spent months agonizing in prayer over a change in job assignments that would move us from Kobe, our home for thirteen years, to Tokyo. Actually, it was a change in jobs for Bernie. I would go along as his wife, even though we had always worked in tandem throughout the twenty years of our marriage.

"You'll always have your writing," Bernie reassured me whenever I worried about my place in Tokyo. Although the decision to move had been made, my agony was growing.

Then all writing doors slammed shut. Silence suddenly reigned. No answers to my prayers. No response to my tears. No insights from the Bible. The harder I searched, the more elusive God became.

Ironically, in the midst of this pain and confusion, I was asked to lead a women's prayer retreat. So it was that I found myself outside that January afternoon. I had instructed the participants to leave the warmth of the conference room for a walk on narrow country lanes that dissected barren rice paddies, accented by terraced mountains, naked persimmon trees, and the familiar tiled roofs of farm houses from which icicles hung in abundance. Our assignment was to find God.

Mufflers wrapped around our faces in response to the sharp wind, we moved out in all directions. My path lead into a thick grove of pine trees. Although several hours of daylight remained, the tall evergreens blocked the sunlight and cloaked my path in darkness. It was an appropriate setting for my troubled spirit.

To my surprise, one bend in the road and I found myself outside

Tarumi Church of God (1967) - *Kobe, Japan*

The work of Tarumi Church of God, in western Kobe, Japan, was launched in 1967 though English classes taught by missionaries Arthur and Norma Eikamp. The first worship service was conducted one year later in the Eikamps' home. Eight people were present—four Eikamps and four Japanese persons. The first Tarumi Church building was built in 1970. Thirty years later, a new building was dedicated in January, 2001.

the trees, engulfed in sunshine. Blinking to adjust to the abrupt brilliance, I discovered a mountain rising from the horizon on my left. Although not a rare sight in Japan, the peak—crowned in misty clouds—was so stunning that I stopped short, neither able to move or to look away.

It was then that God spoke.

"Do you see that mountain?" He asked me.

"Of course," I replied. Despite God's recent silence, it seemed natural to be talking with Him now.

"Do you believe it has a top?" God questioned further.

"Of course," I responded once again.

"But how can you believe it? You can't see the top. It's covered with clouds," He pointed out.

"Mountains always have tops," I answered readily.

"But you can't see it," He persisted.

"That's right," I acknowledged, shrugging my shoulders.

Then God reasoned with me. "If you were to climb that mountain and stand on its summit, you'd know by experience that it's there, right? But until you stand there yourself, you have to accept it by faith."

"I can do that, Lord," I declared easily. Somehow I knew there had to be more to this conversation.

"Then why can't you accept by faith that I have a plan for you in Tokyo—an assignment especially for you?" God spoke powerfully, but gently in His reprimand.

He continued, "Right now you are in Kobe, looking at Tokyo from afar, just as you are viewing that mountain from a distance. I want you to believe I have a plan for you in Tokyo, even as you accept that the mountain peak exists under the cloud through which you cannot see. When you move to Tokyo, you will come to know from your experience what I am asking you now to accept by faith."

My conversation with God lasted only moments. But the results continue to multiply as I exercise faith, trusting God to keep His promise: *"'For I know the plans I have for you,' declares the LORD, 'plans to prosper you and not harm you, plans to give you hope and a future.'" –Jeremiah 29:11*

"...walk in the footsteps of the faith..."
—*Romans 4:12*

My Faith Walk

Ronald O. Hall

t some point in my junior high school years, I had listened enough in church to know that just because my mother was a Christian did not mean I was. I knew I had to confess my sins and turn to Christ on my own. For some reason, this was very difficult for me to do.

There were signs along highways that read something like, "Jesus is coming soon. Will you be ready?" There was a young preacher on the radio named Billy Graham and he made me feel uneasy. There were revivals at our church and at other churches in our community where young people were accepting Christ, but I held back. It got to the point that I would go to bed every night fearful the end of the world would come and I would not be ready. I was fearful, and things I had done wrong, my sins, weighed on my mind. What kept me from going to the altar in church like others was pride and probably not knowing exactly what to say.

Finally, there was another revival at our church and I still did not go forward. I think it was the last night of this meeting, after we got home, that mother said "Ronnie, there is going to be a baptism tomorrow night at the Sixth Avenue Church of God, (Decatur, Alabama). Do you want to be baptized?" Well, the truth was, I did want to, so I said yes.

But I had listened well enough at church to know baptism will not save you. So later on that night, I lay awake in my bed, in a quandary. I did not know what my mother knew about my relationship with God. Maybe she thought I had gone forward that night. But I did indeed wish I had done the necessary thing so I could be appropriately baptized. So I decided right then in my bedroom, by myself, to ask Jesus to save me and come into my life. I do not remember the words I used, but I do remember this removing any anxiety I had about going through with the baptism.

I do not remember if our pastor, Brother Clarence Best, and

Old Sixth Avenue Church of God (1916) - *Decatur, Alabama*

The Sixth Avenue congregation dates its beginning in 1916 but the real beginnings were much earlier. Around 1908, Willis Brown and J. D. Collins held the first revival. A local church was secured for the meeting. The men preached such truth that after three nights they were not permitted to use the church anymore. H. M. Riggle was invited to preach in Decatur. He stirred up curiosity and interest through his wonderful messages. People had a better attitude and a good conception of Church of God teachings.

In 1913, a building was made of cinder blocks which cost ten cents each. Volunteer labor was used with women and children helping in many ways. In 1930, an educational building was added. During 1950 the cinder block building was torn down and a brick sanctuary erected in its place. The sanctuary was completely remodeled in 1965.

I talked about this or not. I do remember waiting in line for him to baptize me and that I walked out the side door of the Sixth Avenue Church of God when it was over, feeling at peace. It was a clear night and the moon and stars seemed somehow to look different than they had before. I thought something like, "Just as I had heard, things really do look different to a Christian." From that point to this day, I have not feared the end of the world.

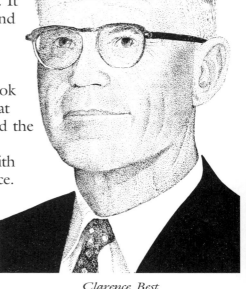

Clarence Best
1902-1963

This experience put me on a faith path I have tried to walk ever since. I have had to confess sins many times over the years and have had to be continually worked on by Him, but I have stayed on the path, going wherever it took me. I am still walking this path, encountering wonderful others along the way, and am committed to staying on it.

The path would lead, over a lifetime, to associations with other Christians in many different contexts. It would affect the choice of a wife, the formation of our family, the development of friendships. I have encountered Christians who inspired me and probably made me a better person by being around them. I have also encountered others trafficking in petty actions and not examples to emulate. I hope I have been in the former category, but suspect at times I have been in the latter.

I would be called upon to serve in local churches on committees and boards, to teach classes and serve in other capacities. In many of these jobs I was poorly prepared, and would have to learn how to do the thing, by *doing the thing*. I have found that teaching a church class is an enormous motivator for Bible study.

I would eventually learn to benefit from grand believers of the past. One commentator I have grown especially fond of is Matthew Henry. I have used his commentary for many years. I also have been influenced by the statements of faith of Corrie Ten Boom, and the victory cadences of Fanny Crosby. I have often read the little devotion book for the days of the year, *Daily Strength for Daily Needs*, compiled by Mary Wilder Tileston.

My faith walk has gone through lonesome valleys, but has been characterized by the fellowship of fellow believers. In the most difficult of times, dear brothers and sisters in Christ have rallied around me, felt my pain, helped me get up and walk again. Their actions placed in my mind the notion that Christ was loving me through them.

I have found that the Christian life is essentially an issue of trust in the love and sovereignty of God, and I am constantly struggling to acquiesce to both. There are major hopes that have not been realized and major disappointments to be lived with. Through it all, there has been a strand of faith that has not been broken. There has been a continuing desire to find and follow the will of God and live an example of the Christian life. I confess this example has not been perfect, but the attempt has persevered.

An enduring element of my faith that has strengthened over the years is the concept of the unity of all believers in Christ. My assessment is that we are much too fragmented over petty issues and doctrines we do not fully understand. We tend to align with scholars of the past to the detriment of the fellowship of the family of God, and the corresponding effect of the gospel on the world. We do not present the world with a whole view of the Body of Christ, rendering it difficult for the world so see Him and His gospel. Therefore, I hope for harmony to come, that brings us faith path travelers together, rendering a lifting up of Christ as never before.

Former pastors of Austinville Church of God:
Sam Germany, Charles Moore, Clarence Best and Ernie Gross

"...great is your faithfulness."
—Lamentations 3:23

In a Church of Bedford Stone

— *Samuel D. Collins*

The church of my childhood and adolescence lingers in my memory. I remember my mother informing me that, at the age of four, I was too young to take communion. As the bread and cup passed by, I folded my arms and indignantly announced, "If I'd known that everybody was going to eat, I would have packed my own lunch!"

I recall my first crush, on a little brown-eyed girl who portrayed Mary in our Christmas pageant. As a lowly shepherd, I had to fight the guilty urge to use my shepherd's crook to whack the kid playing Joseph (or *the Lord's stepfather,* as I thought of him) and make a pass at the mother of Jesus.

I can still feel the chilly water I was baptized in. The church's water heater had gone on the fritz. I emerged from the baptismal pool with chattering teeth and skin the color of a Smurf-blue Crayola.

I can hear the sound of animal-noise imitations echoing off the walls—and rattling the stained-glass windows—after a couple of buddies and I slipped away from a youth party a few houses down the block, made our way into the darkened sanctuary, and cranked up the church PA system as high as it would go. I can also recall the sudden flick of a switch and, as my eyes adjusted to the light, the stern visage of a police officer who had been summoned by the neighbors.

I recall flannel-graph Bible stories; a pre-teen altar commitment made during a weeklong revival; and my first sermon, delivered as a high school student before the home folks (who did their best to pretend they were nodding in agreement as their heads dropped in slumber). Most of all I remember love, support, and encouragement.

In a southern Indiana town, in a church of Bedford stone, I received my first life-changing lessons in Christian commitment, faithfulness, and discipleship. It's not the fault of anyone at New Albany First Church of God that those lessons sometimes took an inordinate amount of time to penetrate my granite-like cranium.

First Church of God (1915) - *New Albany, Indiana*

The New Albany Church began after a revival in Louisville. Many new converts were added among the New Albany people and plans were made for a worship building of their own. In 1929, the little building on Fairmont Avenue had become very crowded. Because of the Depression no one had any money and many did not have work. Firms in the city agreed to furnish materials at a discount. Men who were not working gave full time to the building; those who had jobs worked on the project after work hours. Friends from other churches in town came to help and the carpenter's union sent twenty-one men to help. The building was dedicated in 1931.

When war began in 1942, many new people came to the congregation. A new Bedford stone sanctuary, educaitonal unit and partial basement were dedicated in 1951. In 1957, it became necessary to provide additional classrooms for Sunday school. The area under the sanctuary was excavated and made into classrooms, a choir rehearsal room, restrooms, a small secretarial office and a new furnace room.

"There the LORD *will be our Mighty One.*
It will be like a place of broad rivers and streams."
—Isaiah 33:21

Converted–to God

Kay Murphy Shively

Growing up in the Church of God, I thought I was thoroughly educated in the fine points of the Christian faith. Early into my thirties, however, I began to discern some gaps in my understanding. One of the major, and most troubling, gaps concerned the nature of God. What was God like, and what did God want from me? Salvation, which I had sought at the age of six, had brought me into a *personal relationship with Jesus Christ.* I heard many prayers which began by addressing God, but quickly slid into a conversation with Jesus. I had been taught the doctrine of the Trinity, of course, so presumably God and Jesus were one. At the same time, in the Bible, Jesus seemed to be pointing always beyond himself to God. He said he had come to show us what God was like. The most important law, he said, was that we love God. But I felt a disconnect. From my childhood, I remembered songs about Jesus loving me–and all the children of the world, Jesus wanting me for a sunbeam, and others. Conversely, the song about God that came most quickly to mind exhorted, *"Oh, be careful, little hands, what you do, For the Father up above is looking down in love, So be careful, little hands, what you do."* That verse was followed by warnings to *"Be careful, little eyes, what you see,"* and *"Be careful, little feet, where you go."* God was "looking down in love?" That didn't feel like love to me! The goal of the holiness doctrine I had been taught was perfection. God wanted me to be perfect, I knew, to which end I had sought sanctification. But that again did not seem much like love. How could I love God, be in intimate relationship with God? And how could I know that God loved me?

I learned that other people also found Jesus more friendly, more forgiving, more loving, more approachable than God. I learned that others had this same concept of God as distant and judgmental. God, too, was old; few of us seemed to have outgrown that childhood image of the ancient white-haired man with a long white

United Methodist Church *(The Steeples)*
Camden, Maine

beard sitting on a faraway throne.

For months I struggled to understand how to think about God. "If you've seen me, you've seen God," Jesus had said. If I were to take Jesus seriously, my God-concept needed to grow up.

I cannot tell you exactly where I was when the resolution came; I know I was not in church. To the best of my recollection I was in the car on a trip with my husband. Suddenly, I felt that I was swimming in a wide river, moving comfortably and effortlessly in its flow. The river, I understood, was the universe—God's universe. The river itself was God. And I was in its flow, God's flow; I was in harmony with it, and with God. I was in God. I was enveloped in love. God was loving me, keeping me afloat, keeping me in harmony with God, with the flow of the universe.

This may not be a common metaphor for faith; but it is the metaphor that brought me into relationship with God. I was converted—converted to God.

"Whether you turn to the right or to the left,
your ears will hear a voice behind you, saying, 'This is the way; walk in it.'"
—Isaiah 30:21

Learning to Recognize God's Voice

David E. Markle

Students often ask, "How does one learn to recognize God's voice?" I do not claim to have all wisdom on this subject. It is an important matter. It is a formative concern for our walk with God. Learning to hear and heed God's voice is a crucial discipline for the committed follower of Christ at any age.

One of my best experiences of learning occurred when I ignored what I had heard.

Two friends and I comprised a "witness team" one Sunday morning when we were students. We were to speak at a church in the rolling Indiana countryside. Of course, we did not consult with one another about what each of us planned to speak about. That would have been to hinder the work of the Holy Spirit in directing our course, or so we thought.

As Sunday neared, I asked the Lord what I should prepare to say. A specific text and thought came to mind. I do not recall today what they were. Secure in the knowledge of a message from God to share, I approached the weekend with a minimum of anxiety.

Sunday dawned bright and clear. Crisp, cold air filled our lungs as we loaded into John's car. The fields of corn and beans harvested months prior, now flocked with a dusting of freshly-fallen snow, sped by as we quickly made the fifteen-mile drive to the church. On the way, my anxiety level heightened: Would my message be of any value to the people? Would what I had to say fit well with the words of my friends? Would I look bad because my witness had less impact than that of my cohorts? With these fears swirling in my brain and my uncertain heart pounding, I made a hasty decision to switch my topic and text and speak about something that at the moment "made more sense."

White Union Christian Church (1872)
near Sulphur Springs, Indiana

Known at first as New Light Church, White Union Christian Church was founded on March 30, 1878. The first pastor was Dr. D. C. Misener. The church originally sat on the south side of U.S. Highway 36. In 1881, George and Sarah Fleming gave the ground on which the church now stands. The property was given with the stipulation that it be used on the third Saturday and Sunday of the month by the Christian Church. At other times it was to be used by the Old School Baptists. The original building was thirty-two feet by forty feet and cost $1,000. Classrooms were added in 1910 and 1912.

After we had spoken and the service had ended, the people were very kind and supportive. They affirmed our fledgling efforts. In my heart, I knew that what I had said had paled next to what I might have said. What I might have said was the message that God had given me earlier in the week. It fit perfectly with the thoughts of my friends. Since I spoke in the middle, it would have knitted our three-fold efforts as one. Its expression would have taught me a valuable lesson about hearing and heeding God's voice. But our resourceful Lord taught me a lifelong lesson anyway.

As you can tell, I have forgotten some of the details of that morning. But I have never forgotten that sense of certainty that will not be shaken when I have heard from God. There is a peace that abides within when I have prayerfully and carefully listened for the Lord's direction and that direction has come. There is a confidence that is beyond myself when I speak and act in concert with our Lord's direction.

Recently, I have taken on a significant preaching responsibility. Our first weeks together were concerned with working through a New Testament book. As it progressed, I began to think and pray on what should come next. I consulted a lectionary and began to work with upcoming passages of Scripture. It did not seem that the Lord was working in my efforts. As I continued to pray, the fertile fields of John, chapters 14 to 16 came to mind. They promised resources that I perceived we needed as a people. Amidst this season, several persons in our congregation faced the loss of loved ones. Our community shared in the national shock of the events of September 11, 2001. More than once in this series, we found ourselves exactly where we needed to be in the *paraclete* passages of John's Gospel.

This recent experience witnesses to the matchless adequacy of God's Word. But it also reminds me of an experience of God's guidance—ignored—in a small, country church so many years ago. I am still profiting from that lesson of God's guidance, ignored. It taught me something about how to recognize our Lord's voice, that voice, indescribable yet unmistakable in its tone.

"Trust in the LORD with all your heart and lean not on your own understanding..."
—Proverbs 3:5

Certain Knowledge

Gertrude E. Wunsch

In catechism class I learned that "faith is a certain knowledge and a hearty trust." The verses in Proverbs 3:5-6 *"Trust in the LORD with all your heart and lean not on your own understanding; in all your ways acknowledge him, and he will make your paths straight,"* pertain to my personal faith. In my teenage days a dear man in our church took the young people to Soldiers Field in Chicago. A godly man from California, Charles E. Fuller, founder of Fuller Seminary, was coming to speak. It was a time of inner assessment and commitment to the Lord.

Hebrews 11 gives excellent reassurance. The first verse in this chapter says: *"Now faith is being sure of what we hope for and certain of what we do not see."* The challenge from Charles E. Fuller to me personally was given. I had personally accepted the Lord, but would often have doubts of the future. Some simple examples of God's gifts continued to help my understanding and belief. *"Believe in the Lord Jesus, and you will be saved." –Acts 16:31*

Believe in the ring buoy as it is tossed to you in dire need in deep water. Reach for it. It will hold you up. You must believe when you grab it. It will save you.

Hebrews 11:6 says it all—*"And without faith it is impossible to please God, because anyone who comes to him must believe that he exists and that he rewards those who earnestly seek him."*

Hebrews 11 is a wonderful example of all God's people who by faith followed God's commands: Noah, Abraham, Jacob, Joseph, Moses, Gideon, Barak, Samson, Jephthah, David, Samuel and the prophets, who through faith conquered kingdoms.

God's promise in Hebrews 13, verses 5, 6 and 8 is a wonderful assurance, for He said *"'...Never will I leave you, never will I forsake you.' So we say with confidence, 'The Lord is my helper; I will not be afraid. Jesus Christ is the same yesterday and today and forever.'"*

Thank you, Lord, for your promises. "My faith looks up to Thee, author of liberty."

First Church of Christ (1638) - *Sandwich, Massachusetts*

The worship history of the First Church of Christ in Sandwich can be traced back to 1638. All Cape Cod towns were founded by people unhappy with the Boston-area Puritans. The religious history of Sandwich like all New England towns, has taken many twists and turns depending on the economy, history and the winds of change.

The present building was decided on in 1847 to accommodate enlarging membership. Its spire design is often spoken of as reminscent of the London spires designed by Christopher Wren.

"...I urge you,...in view of God's mercy, to offer your bodies as living sacrifices, holy and pleasing to God—this is your spiritual act of worship."
—Romans 12:1 NRSV

Complete Surrender

Gilbert W. Stafford

I was sitting at the table with two dear friends, John and Delores Long, in Brookings, South Dakota. I had stood up with him at their wedding in Brookings, her hometown. Now John was serving as pastor in the same congregation. It had been decades since we had eaten together. Immediately after the table grace, John's first words were a question: "Gil, do you remember the prayer of consecration we prayed when we were students at Anderson College?"

This question led us into further reflection about the significance of what we did that night. It was in Room 224 of Dunn Hall that John and I, along with two other friends, knelt and offered prayers of total surrender to the Lord. We prayed for each other and then each of us prayed a personal prayer in the presence of the others. We did not know what the Lord had in mind for us, but whatever it was we wanted to be completely surrendered to it. All of us had grown up hearing Romans 12:1 preached and taught: *"...present your bodies as a living sacrifice, holy and acceptable to God, which is your spiritual worship."* We had been nurtured by the many songs in the rich consecration tradition, songs like Mildred Howard's, *Consecration* the refrain of which rang in our hearts and minds: *"My life, O Lord, I give to Thee, My talents, time and all; I'll serve Thee, Lord, and faithful be, I'll hear Thy faintest call."* We had read and heard persons like E. Stanley Jones, the great missionary to India and guest on the Anderson campus, emphasizing this theme. And now it was time for us to come to the decisive moment as to what we were going to do about it.

John and I talked about how definitive for our whole lives those prayers that night had been. For many years, every card in my billfold carried the letters "c.s." after my name, a constant reminder of that experience of complete surrender.

While John's ministry has taken one expression, and mine another, in each case the prayers in Room 224 were being lived out. Time

Troy Presbyterian Church (1874) - *Troy, Kentucky*

The history of Troy Presbyterian Church has been a history of church unions. Since the earliest pioneer days, separate congregations in the area have felt God's call to unite. In 1841, the church was re-organized as an Associate Reformed Church. For a number of years prior to this time several churches were begun and either closed or united with others. In 1874, a union congregation was organized as Troy Presbyterian Church. Land in Troy was purchased and a new brick building was erected.

An interesting feature of the union was the provision for the singing of Psalms. Many Protestant churches before the 18th century held that Psalms were the only proper form of church music. A compromise was effected whereby one Psalm would be sung in the Sunday worship service.

after time in my own life when decisions about my life and ministry were being made by me and by others, the living out of this complete surrender has been predominate. I confess that at times I have found it difficult to figure out the ways of God and of the people of God, but in every case I have fallen back on the prayer of complete surrender and have reiterated it in each new circumstance of life, sincerely believing that the Lord is faithful and that ultimately He is in control of my life. As 2 Timothy 1:12 says: *"I know the one in whom I have put my trust, and I am sure that he is able to guard until that day what I have entrusted to him."* That has always been a completely sufficient perspective during those times when human perspectives were so inadequate.

Consecration

Mildred E. Howard, 1907

Andrew L. Byers, 1869-1952

1 Since Je - sus gave his life for me Should I not give him mine?
2 I care not where my Lord di-rects, His pur - pose I'll ful - fill;
3 My home and friends are dear to me, Yet he is dear-er still;
4 My all, O Lord, to thee I give, Ac - cept it as thine own;

I'm con - se - crat - ed, Lord, to thee, I shall be whol - ly thine.
I know he ev - ery one pro-tects Who does his ho - ly will.
In my af - fec - tion first he'll be, And first his right-eous will.
For thee a - lone I'll ev - er live, My heart shall be thy throne.

REFRAIN

My life, O Lord, I give to thee, My tal - ents, time and all; I'll

serve thee, Lord, and faith-ful be, I'll hear thy faint-est call. A-men.
faint-est call.

"Now to him who is able to do immeasurably more than all we ask or imagine,
according to His power that is at work within us, to him be glory..."
—*Ephesians 3:20-21*

To the Very Last Drop

Robert E. Edwards

The middle of 1970 until the end of that decade were very difficult years to live in Tanzania. The government was preparing for war with Idi Amin's Uganda; the land was parched dry by a three-year drought; and the Tanzanian government was experimenting with a failed form of African Socialism. The result was that life was very hard. Everything was rationed: flour, rice, sugar, TP, LP gas, diesel, petrol. Everything. The village of Mbulu, where we lived, formed a committee that sat to *fairly* distribute whatever came into the town. Long lines of persons with needs formed on a dusty, back street leading into a rickety wooden door where the committee sat daily behind a large wooden desk. Our small Bible school was not a very high priority on their acquisition list. We always seemed to get whatever was left over.

When our storage of diesel finally gave out we began to use kerosene lamps at the school and in our home instead of the generator. And our supply of petrol became frighteningly low. I hid back just enough for my Landcruiser to get us to the nearest larger town of Arusha, some five hours down a very rough dirt road. This is where we would have to go for major medical help, to purchase what groceries were available, and hopefully, where we might be able to buy some more petrol for the trip back to Mbulu.

Late one night there came a knock on the door. As my lamp lit the faces of the two young men standing outside, I immediately recognized the grave concern on their faces. As they told me their story, I knew that I was being tested as to our compassion for others and our own personal needs. The young wife of one of the men was having her first child, but it was coming breech, and she needed immediate medical help from our rural hospital. The husband pleaded in his broken Swahili, "Tafadhali, uje nasi kumchukua na

Murray Church of God (1958)
Mama Isara, Mbulu, Tanzania

Murray Church of God was begun in 1958 through the efforts of Stan and Marion Hoffman, Ralph and Gertie Farmer and Roy and Magaline Hoops. These couples faced much hardship in planting churches under the most difficult conditions among the Wambugwe, the Wairaqw and the Wabarunge.

Bob and Jan Edwards came to Tanzania in their first missionary assignment in 1972 to live and minister in Mbulu. Bob was the principal of a small rural Swahili Bible School.

Today Yoeli Dirangw pastors the Murray Church of God.

kumpelekea kwa hospitali." (Please, come with us to get her and take her to the hospital.) What to do?

Jan and I talked it over. If I went with them in the car, I would have to use the last of our petrol, and our way out of possible troubles. If I refused, the woman would probably die. As we looked at their worried faces, we knew that we really didn't have a choice. We had to help the woman. So we prayed. "Father, You know our predicament. We cannot say no to these young men who have come a long distance to ask for help. So we ask You to help get this young woman to the hospital, and spare her life. And we will just have to depend on You to answer the problem of more fuel. Amen." I filled the car's tank and drove into the night, not returning until early the next morning. Doctors at the hospital helped the woman deliver her first child, and both the mother and the child were well. But my tank was dry. I parked the car to the side of the house, knowing that it would not be going anywhere for some time.

Then something wonderful happened. At the end of that very week, news came to us of an unexpected fuel tanker that had come into the town. That afternoon our telephone rang, and I was told to come to collect my two hundred liters of petrol, more than double the amount that I had requested from the committee weeks earlier. I do believe that sometimes our heavenly Father allows us to go to the very end of our limits to measure our faith in Him, and to see how we will react in those crisis situations. It is always for our good. And He knows our needs even before we ask. For He "...*is able to do immeasurably more than all we ask or imagine, according to his power that is at work within us.*"–*Ephesians 3:20*

*"I will lift up my eyes to the mountains; From whence shall my help come?
My help comes from the Lord, Who made heaven and earth.
He will not allow your foot to slip; He who keeps you will not slumber."
—Psalm 121:1-3 NASB*

We're Going
to Climb This
Mountain Together

Sylvia Kennedy Grubbs

ost people do not know it, but I am a mountain climber. I'm not very athletic. I'm not very brave or strong, but I am an experienced *life* mountain climber.

Mountains are awesome symbols of God at work–beautiful snow-capped peaks and vistas, high and rocky, time-scarred cliffs. They call me to the presence of our almighty, powerful God. He is always calling my name, saying, "Trust Me in and through these mountain journeys. I am with you. I am taking you to a higher place." Recently, I wrote in my journal on September 24, 4:24 A.M., 2001:

"Lord, we can't climb this mountain by ourselves. The very deepest part of me cries out. I can't give her up, yet, not my will. My sweet, sweet sissy, my flesh, my friend, my light, my support through it all. Unconditional love and beauty always–gifts beyond measure–pretty things–little surprises left on my bed, in my heart–always giving–always loving–always lifting.

Oh Lord, we're down here in this valley and all I can say is we're in a fog, visibility almost none. So what do we do? Occasionally we see a lifting, the sun peeks through. Our spirits, our faith–strong, and then the fog rolls in again. For now, we are just numb–wandering around down here in the fog, and it's scary, Lord. Hold our hands–let's make a chain–loved ones and friends, blessed church. Pick her up–we'll carry her! Lord, we can see Your face! You are right here with us–hovering over all of us–Your great arms of mercy and compassion, all the way. Slowly we're moving–moving up the

St. Isidores Catholic Church
Las Animas County near Weston, Colorado

mountain and the elevation is changing. You will lead us–all the way up this mountain!

Perhaps it will be the most difficult of all our trips–yet–somehow I believe, beautiful. Lord, you will be our *way*, our *truth*, our *light*, the essential necessities for our trip. Faith, perseverance and hope we will carry; we don't need any more luggage. But we're leaving some room. I have a feeling we'll pick up some things along our way.

Lord, I don't know how long this trip will take us. We've taken these cancer trips before and yes, they are long and they aren't easy. But then, you never said, 'This is the easy way, go here.' You have prepared for us and given the instructions–for this unknown journey ahead. So we are headed for the top–lift us up–carry us high! *"I will lift up my eyes to the mountains; From whence shall my help come? My help comes from the LORD, Who made heaven and earth. He will not allow your foot to slip; He who keeps you will not slumber."* –Psalm 121:1-3 *NASB*

I said to sister the first day, 'We're going to climb this mountain together!' *"...Come, let us go up to the mountain of the LORD....He will teach us his ways, so that we may walk in his paths...."* –Isaiah 2:3 *"LORD, you have been our dwelling place throughout all generations. Before the mountains were born...from everlasting to everlasting you are God."* –Psalm 90:1-2

Our compassionate Lord, thank you, for your promises to us. *"'Though the mountains be shaken and the hills be removed, yet my unfailing love for you will not be shaken nor my covenant of peace be removed,' says the LORD, who has compassion on you."* –Isaiah 54:10 *"...He is my refuge and my fortress, my God, in whom I trust. He will cover you with his feathers, and under his wings you will find refuge; his faithfulness will be your shield and rampart. You will not fear the terror of night,...For he will command his angels concerning you to guard you in all your ways."* –Psalm 91:2, 4-5, 11

Thank you, thank you, our Savior, our Lord, Jesus Christ, who was before us, is with us, and is forever eternal above us–yet–in us. Oh, divine miracle!

P.S. It is now November. We are still climbing with my sister Lita! Along with the changes, challenges and surprises, our merciful Lord has given so many blessings.

"...Woman, you have great faith!'"
—Matthew 15:28

The Church

Wayne R. Gordon

he church. What do those words conjure up in *your* mind? Is it a little one room white frame building on East Vine Street? Is it a stately red brick with white pillars on Highway 11? If you are like me you have heard those words all your life. "It's time to get ready for church." "Hurry up we'll be late for church!" "We have to get there early to build the fire in the wood stove so it will be warm for church." I read my dad's *Thompson Chain Reference Bible* cover to cover there, well maybe I read the covers and looked at the maps but, if the doors were open we were at *the church*.

As a boy, *the church* was a focal point of my life. All my friends, except Andrew Jackson Patton, he was a Presbyterian, went to *the church*. Most of my mentors were at *the church*, including Myrtle Smith, mother of Tom A. Smith. She played the piano. She could play from memory any Church of God hymn on

Myrtle Evangeline Stumpt Smith
1886-1983

that tinny old upright. She could also pray. Oh could she pray! Wednesday night prayer meeting at 7:30 P.M., on our knees, on

St. Paul's Catholic Church (1836) - St. Paul, Oregon

A group of French and Indian fur traders employed by the Hudson Bay Company were seeking spiritual guidance. They called upon Father Blanchet. He came and began to work in the area. The first mass was held in 1839. The church was built in 1846 and is the oldest in the state of Oregon. Father Blanchet later became an archbishop.

wood floors and wood pews, it seemed it was an eternity, she would pray for wisdom from God, but most of all she would pray for the youth of *the church*, out loud, by name!

Myrtle Smith prayed for me, sometimes I didn't want her to, because it was like she had a window to look into my heart. When she prayed, her voice was as though it came from a higher place, a place that had special meaning and authority. She lived a simple life committed to leading others to Christ. *The church* was central in her life and her example was always before me, her countenance was always beside me, and her nudging support was always behind me.

The church was at first a building; it became a place; then it was a destination; but most of all it was the people. There was not a *flash moment* that led me to commit to a path that would always bring me to *the church*. Rather, it was the quality, the commitment, and the perseverance, regardless of the obstacles, of these people that made *the church* live in my life. I became aware that there was a difference in the people at *the church*. That difference was a love of Christ that had no boundary.

Those maps in the back of that Bible showed the travels of Christ, the Israelites, Paul, and the development of the early church. It was the day by day travel in the Christian life of a diminutive woman of God, casting such a large shadow of persistent loving care, that was a turning point of my life, in my journey, in *the church*.

"But because of his great love for us, God, who is rich in mercy,
made us alive with Christ even when we were dead in
our transgressions—it is by grace you have been saved."
—Ephesians 2:4-5

The Heart of Faith

William E. Ferguson

Grace! I've heard it spoken of since I was a child. I was told to accept it by faith in pre-adolescence. I studied its etymology in seminary. I have preached on the theme many times. Yet, there are things that are not fully understood without encountering them face to face.

During high school, I was the number one player on the varsity basketball team. Even though I enjoyed a measure of popularity, I struggled to feel confident, capable and valued. Oh, my parents and family loved me, the church loved me, but for some reason the approval of my school friends was very important at that time.

One Friday night after a game, I attended a party with my teammates. As I left the party, I accidentally popped the clutch of the car I was driving and tapped the rear bumper of the car parked in front of me. I took a quick glance at what I considered to be nothing but a scratch and then I drove home. I thought the incident was behind me and no harm had been done, until the following Monday after basketball practice. My father met me in the driveway as I got out of the car. He greeted me by saying, "David's father called and said you hit and ruined the rear bumper of his restored 1968 Buick Riviera at a party last Friday night. The damage is $300.00!"

At that moment, my life flashed before me. It was clear that I had been at a party without my parents' approval. It was clear that I had an accident and didn't mention it. It was clear to me that my life was over. As far as I could imagine, the penalty would be nothing short of death!

What my dad did and what he said, after my weak attempt to explain, was amazing. He turned to me and said with compassion, "We'll take care of it." Then, we walked into the house. My parents didn't speak a word of the incident after that moment. I was stunned

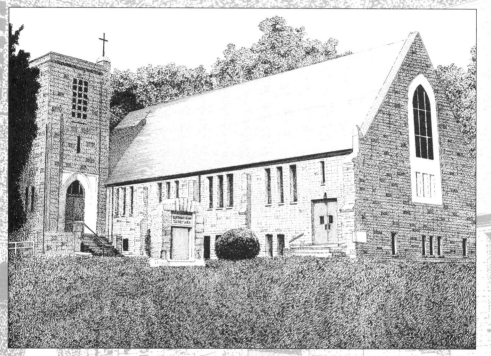

National Memorial Church of God (1916) - *Washington, D.C.*

National Memorial Church of God began as a fellowship of believers in 1917. The church met in various homes and in a storefront in northeast D.C. until a new building was completed in 1942 at its present location. Esther Boyer Bauer gave pastoral direction and supervision to the construction project. National Memorial became a rallying point for raising funds in children's ministries, youth groups, women's missionary societies and the like, across the Church of God in North America. The Board of Church Extension, the Gospel Trumpet Company, and other agencies heralded the call for a building to be built that would be a symbol of the Church of God in the nation's capital. This was not an uncommon occurrence across the major denominations and faith groups in the early 1900s. During Campmeeting in Anderson from 1937 through 1942 bricks were sold to raise funds.

The most prominent feature of the building is a large stained-glass window in the chancel depicting Jesus surrounded by people of every age, from the different nations and tribes of the world. The building currently houses an English-speaking congregation of over ten nationalities, a Spanish-speaking congregation from many nations and a Creole-speaking congregation from Haiti. All are Church of God congregations.

by their response. I didn't expect it. I didn't fully understand it. I didn't deserve it.

I have reflected back on that moment in my life many times. There are daily situations in life that grace can transform: a fender bent, a disappointing decision made, a promise broken, an expectation unfulfilled, an offense intended or unintended. I was confronted by grace! Now, I am trying to live a grace-filled life. Grace saves. Grace delivers. Grace heals. Grace restores. It is the heart of faith. By God's grace, in and through us, amazing and life-changing things happen.

The Window Speaks

At last the dream for a place of worship for the Church of God in Washington, D.C., was being realized. With great joy we saw the stone and other materials being laid on the lot at 16th and Taylor NW. 16th Street was one of the busiest streets leading from the White House passing our location to the Army and Navy Hospitals and other government buildings.

One of the decisions that had to be made was the selection of a theme for the chancel window facing 16th Street, that would be seen by many passing commuters. The architect's plan was for a three-panel window tied together by a single theme, and framed with beautiful Indiana limestone. The center panel would be 13 feet high, and each side panel 8 feet high.

I recall vividly the serious excitement of the planning committee as we faced, the key question, "What message will this window speak?" A story that I had heard gave us some guidance. It told about an artist who was commissioned to design a church window depicting "Jesus and the Children." He gave his heart to the work, and at last it was finished. The next day it would be presented for acceptance.

That night when he retired, his last thought was about the design he had created. Then he had a terrifying dream. Someone was in his studio, standing before his picture with brush in hand, altering it. "You have ruined my picture," he cried. "Who told you my children were all white?"

This story caught the imagination of our committee, and we decided the children of the world would be represented as well as persons of various ages. When the initial art work was done and submitted, it was beautiful–from the tiny baby to the feeble elderly, many races and ages represented.

As the building work progressed, the crisis of Pearl Harbor on December 7 broke. Washington was in turmoil. Tension, fear, and anger were rampant. We closed our Sunday evening service with prayer. In the midst of this, the plan for our window was questioned, and someone suggested that we leave the Oriental (Japanese) figure out. I still shudder in fear as I think about that. We went ahead with our original plan. If not, the window would have been a monument to prejudice, slight, and hate.

Today that window still speaks. It proclaims that all persons are loved of God–race or age make no difference. A spotlight from within the church brings that message to all who pass by, even at night. So let the window speak–Jesus, the Savior of the world and the Savior of every age–blessed be the name of the Lord.

Esther Boyer Bauer (1905-1988)
Former pastor of the National Memorial Church of God

"...Because you have so little faith. I tell you the truth, if you have faith as small as a mustard seed, you can say to this mountain, 'Move from here to there' and it will move. Nothing will be impossible for you."
—Matthew 17:20

A Grain of Mustard Seed

Annalou Deese Espey

It was January of 1945 when we arrived at Anderson College, the great promised land. We came so that Joe, my husband who had felt his call for ministry, could attend college. I supported him wholeheartedly. Even though snow had been on the ground since Thanksgiving, we were eager to park our little trailer and get on with the expectations that were ahead. There were no places equipped for parking a trailer but the college let us park behind what is now Byrum Hall, the Old Tabernacle.

College Haven - 1948

Since we had no bathroom or running water in our trailer, the facilities in the gym came in real handy. Our little home was nestled under a big oak tree that still stands today these many years later. We had only fifteen dollars, did not know even one person, and our

223

The Old Tabernacle/Gymnasium (1908) - *(Byrum Hall)*
Anderson University, *Anderson, Indiana*

Byrum Hall was the first permanent tabernacle erected in Anderson by the Church of God after it had brought general headquarters to Anderson in 1906. With the assistance of a grant from Lily Endowment, Inc., the structure, dating from 1908, was renovated in 1974 and is home for Anderson University drama programs.

little baby girl was whooping with whooping cough. She survived with the aid of old-fashioned remedies.

It was time for the second semester to begin. Joe went to the Registrar's Office to let them know that he was here to go to college. He had not known that he was supposed to have pre-registered. He passed the entrance examination but was informed that he should take the *bonehead* English class without credit. This class proved to be the most beneficial class of his college career.

There were times when we did not know where the next meal was coming from, and then there would come a big box from my parents who pastored in South Carolina, a big box containing smoked ham, cornmeal and potatoes! Joe did all sorts of jobs—like washing windows in the old, palatial homes of Edgewood. The first Christmas we were here, he had a chance to make a little money by taking some students to Alabama for the holidays, where he could also visit his mother and sister, Ann. He took our daughter, Marcie, who was fourteen months old with him. I stayed in someone's room in Old Main and worked the switchboard. Helen Holton had told me that I could work through the holidays. Thankfully, that job then lasted through our stay at the college. Dr. and Mrs. Cecil Hartselle invited me to Christmas dinner. I shall never forget that gesture of kindness.

Another time, one hundred dollars came through the mail from a cousin, by the way of Joe's mother. He said that he felt like Joe needed some money. Much to our sorrow, that cousin was killed in a mine accident a couple of months later.

There were anxious moments during these college years, such as when Joe was called into the office of a college executive, and told that we could no longer live by the Old Tabernacle. Joe told me that we would have to go home. I told him that we were not going to go home. I went to the executive's office and told him that we were not moving because Joe had come here to go to college. There was not much discussion after he found out that my parents were ministers. We did not move and that was truly a turning point in our life, in our journey of mustard seed faith. I hate to think what would have happened if we had left. We can never thank Anderson College, now Anderson University, enough for what happened in our lives!

"*...and nothing shall be impossible unto you.*"

"And we know that in all things God works for the good of those who love him, who have been called according to his purpose."
—Romans 8:28

Finding Faith in the Process

Jerry C. Grubbs

"Dad, when I go to the bathroom, it's all red. What does that mean?" asked our eight-year-old son as he sat down for dinner one evening. Keith was a typical energetic and active eight-year-old and had just come in for dinner following a community sandlot football game. The football game and the events following that dinner time question taught me a never forgotten lesson about prayer and faith.

Things moved quite rapidly the next morning. An examination by our family physician was followed by immediate referral for extensive X-rays at the hospital. By mid-morning, doctors were scurrying and conferring with each other. The first report that came to us was, "Your son might have cancer." Needless to say, we heard few of the other explanations, only the feared red-flag word *cancer*.

Further examinations and tests by a specialist, with consultation from other urologists, pinpointed the problem. Keith did not have cancer at all, but rather a rare third kidney that had grown and ballooned out of control. A tackle during the football game had signaled the problem. At the time of the football injury, the abnormal kidney had destroyed half of his left kidney, fused itself to the bladder and caused considerable damage to other internal organs.

The surgeon (one of the best according to our family doctor) informed us that a three-hour operation was required to remove the growth and repair damage to internal organs. As we had so often done, our family and surrounding friends placed Keith and the doctors in God's hands for the three-hour operation. With our faith supported by loving family and friends, we waited. Four hours into the surgery the surgeon, our family doctor and the assisting doctor emerged from the operation room. We thought, "Finally, it's over."

Big Lake Church of God (1917) - *Columbia City, Indiana*

In 1917, a group of neighbors began gathering for cottage prayer meetings. Most of these meetings were held in a lake cottage on the Joseph Ravick farm. At these prayer meetings the leadership gradually fell to Miss Mamie Surfus.

When the church was organized in 1918, she became the first pastor. The first church was dedicated on July 12, 1920. It was built by labors of love and time from the congregation, and rich blessing from God. Men, women, and children went out in the fields and gathered stones for the foundation and basement.

"How did it go?" I asked. The surgeon's reply took the wind out of my faith. "It was a good stopping point," he replied, "so we thought we would take a break."

I guess I had enough faith for a three-hour operation...but what now? Finally, after another four hours, the surgeon came out again and explained that the problem was much more extensive than the X-rays had revealed. The surgeon had removed half of the left kidney, disconnected the ureter from the bladder and attempted to fuse it to the bladder again. "With all the damage done to his internal organs, Keith will probably never be able to father children," the specialist said in a rather routine and stoic manner.

After a long stay in the hospital, Keith went home on the first of November wearing a surgically implanted drainage system—tube and bag. The urologist explained that he would have to wear this for a year or more to enable the damaged kidney and other organs to heal properly. Care of such a system on an eight-year-old was no small matter. And we prayed often that God would give us patience and even asked God to intervene and heal his frail body. But, as the days passed, our patience and our faith wore thin.

Thanksgiving Day of that year was a special time for us. We were celebrating the day with several families in our friendship circle. As we prepared for dinner, Keith sat down on my lap to catch his breath from playing with the other children. As I had done so many times, I automatically reached to check the bag on his drainage system and discovered that the bag was totally empty. I asked if he had just emptied it. "No, Daddy," he said. "I haven't emptied it since last night." The urologist had warned us that if the bag was empty it probably was not functioning properly and Keith would be in danger of poisioning himself internally.

We rushed to the hospital emergency room where the doctor on duty examined him. The specialist who had done the surgery was out of town for the holiday. However, we were assured that there was no sign of internal drainage and that Keith appeared in no danger. I explained to Keith that the drainage had stopped, that there was some kind of difficulty and that we would have to come back to the hospital the next day when the specialist returned. Keith took my arm and pulled me close. "Well, Daddy," he said, "isn't this what we've been praying for all this time?" A little child shall lead them!

The next morning, the specialist ran a complete set of X-rays and with a puzzled look on his face explained to us that the healing process which was to take a year or more was suddenly complete. Keith did not need the external drainage system any longer. Internal organs were fully restored and functioning as the Master Creator designed them.

And, a resounding exclamation point was added to this miracle twenty-four years later. Keith, along with his beautiful wife, Elizabeth, gave birth in 1997 to Olivia, our granddaughter—God's miracle child.

Whenever our prayers are seemingly not answered immediately or within our own timing, we can learn that faith often comes not in the immediate circumstances, but in the process. I have learned the important lesson that "...*in all things, God is working for the good of those who love Him.*" In all things...a football game that signaled in a timely way a problem that needed to be addressed; Christian doctors who offered their human knowledge to the Great Physician for His use; a young body marvelously created with restorative powers within it; and family and friends who sustained us in difficult times, when we could not find the spiritual resources to trust the process; and joyously, the gift of fathering a child.

"I can do everything through him who gives me strength."
—Philippians 4:13

Belevedere

Dondeena Fleenor Caldwell

Getting married not only meant changing my last name and residence, but also my language. From a social worker in Indiana, I became the wife of Maurice Caldwell, pastor of a Spanish-speaking congregation in Belvedere (East Los Angeles), California.

Through pantomime and broken Spanish, I could manage to communicate, but listening to Maurice's sermons was another story. By the time I translated a word in my mind, I would discover that I was two paragraphs behind him. Every Sunday I went home next door to the little frame parsonage with a headache from so much concentration and frustration. Whenever possible, Maurice would take me to a nearby church's prayer service in English so I could feel spiritually fed.

The women's sewing circle was the perfect place for a pastor's wife to serve as the spiritual advisor. Since that was out of the question for this non-Spanish-speaking spouse, I decided that at least I could do a superb job embroidering tea towels. Imagine my chagrin when I discovered that I had embroidered right through to my skirt! When would I ever be worthy of these women's acceptance?

That's why I was surprised when Sister Carlin told Maurice that she, who spoke no English, would like for me to spend a day in her home. She took me through her garden, naming every flower and plant, in Spanish. She introduced me to her neighbors, in Spanish. We toured her humble home while she described each picture or object, in Spanish. Then she sat me down with a magazine, in Spanish, while she prepared a delicious Mexican meal.

When Maurice came to take me back to the parsonage, Sister Carlin gave me a warm hug and baptized me in more Spanish. Words and phrases swirled through my head as we drove home, almost as if the pump had been primed. A few weeks later, I stood in church to say my first Bible verse in Spanish. Sister Carlin beamed at me as I said, "Todo lo puedo en Cristo que me fortalece" ("I can do all things through Christ who strengthens me").

Belvedere Church of God (1931) - *Los Angeles, California*

The first service was held on June 14, 1931. A. T. Mayfield was the first pastor. The Belvedere Church was the first Spanish-speaking church in the Church of God. Maurice Caldwell was the second pastor of the church.

"Wise men store up knowledge, but the mouth of a fool invites ruin."
—Proverbs 10:14

Life-Changing Experience

John A. Morrison

On my eighteenth birthday I underwent a life-changing experience. My stepbrother, Earl L. Martin, and I accepted Jesus Christ as our Savior. It happened in a one-room country schoolhouse on Benton Creek in the back woods of Crawford County, Missouri. Reverend and Mrs. James Trask, a young sincere couple, were the traveling evangelists.

In the early 1900s, my grandfather, John Henry Morrison, found a discarded *Gospel Trumpet* along side a country road. He felt inspired to write the editor of the paper, because he liked what he had read. The editor's name was Daniel S. Warner. At my grandfather's invitation, D. S. Warner and his singers came to preach in the area.

John Henry Morrison subscribed to the *Gospel Trumpet.* I heard the stories of D. S. Warner from my grandfather all during my boyhood. This spiritual influence ignited the fire and desire to dedicate my life to the Lord and commit myself to the newly-founded Church of God, which had no building, but proclaimed a message that thrilled my soul.

I announced that I was sure that God wanted me to become a preacher. After my marriage to the beautiful and devoted Eunice Drennen, and Earl Martin's marriage to the charming Blanche Williams, we went around the Ozark countryside into any church or school that would allow us to sing and I would preach.

My ability as a young preacher led me to Hurricane Ridge, West Virginia, as an assistant to Reverend Trask. In 1914, when their first child was born, he was named Earl in honor of my beloved stepbrother.

Eunice and I worked and learned for three years in West Virginia and then received an invitation to my first full-time pastorate in Delta, Colorado. We stayed in Delta for a year and a half. Then in

First Church of God (1887) - *St. James, Missouri*

In the early 1880s many people in the environs of St. James held to the doctrines advocated by the Gospel Trumpet. *John Henry Morrison, grandfather of John A. Morrison, heard that D. S. Warner was setting out on an evangelistic tour. He wrote to Warner and asked him to stop at St. James. Early on the morning of July 28, 1887, he went to the train depot, expecting to meet the train with Warner and his team. As he approached the depot he heard strains of what seemed to him to be the most heavenly music he had ever heard coming from the old hotel. He was told by a bystander that his people had come the night before at 12:30. They were seated around the breakfast table singing. A hall was secured in town for that night and a large crowd attended the services.*

The first Church of God building was erected in 1904 and stood where the old city jail had been. In the spring of 1937, ground was broken for a new basement which was used for worship until a sanctuary was completed in 1948. It was made from native sandstone and is one of the most beautiful churches in that section of Missouri.

1917, a life-changing letter arrived from J. T. Wilson of Anderson, Indiana. The letter was inviting me to come to the Anderson Bible Training School of the Church of God as the administrative teacher. J. T. Wilson was going to be the manager of the Gospel Trumpet Company, the printing branch of the Church of God.

I accepted the invitation with excitement and trepidation. Our family left Colorado and our loving congregation for the 1690 mile trip to Indiana. We left in an old open Model T Ford with a five-year-old boy and a six-month-old baby girl.

This traveling experience brought us our share of challenges. We were stuck in snow, stranded in mud, drenched with rain, caught in a flash flood. We ferried rivers and changed tires. We were dirty, hungry, sleepy, deadbroke and caring for

John A. Morrison
1893-1965

two little babies; but we were convinced that God had a purpose for our lives in Anderson. My formal education extended only to the completion of the eighth grade. I was largely self-taught. I suffered years of ill health; yet, with God's help, met the challenge of a career in education.

During my thirty-nine years as president of Anderson College, I was able to combine my natural gifts as a persuasive speaker with my ability to be an administrator with a passion for Christian higher education. Through much prayer and perseverance we built a small struggling Bible school into an accredited Christian college.

*"...they who seek the LORD will praise him—
may your hearts live forever!"*
—Psalm 22:26

Golden Hearts in the Family of God

Janetta Hitt Slattery

In the late 1950s, doctors at Riley Children's Hospital in Indianapolis were doing groundbreaking heart surgery on young children. For a short time, they were replacing valves in defective hearts with gold ones. They had found that the only metal blood would not clot to was gold. When my husband Phil was seven, he had that very experimental operation, and it saved his life. People with a kind, generous nature are described as having a *heart of gold*. For Phil this was true in a figurative and literal sense.

In his adult years, Phil was a teddy bear of a man with hugs to match. In his work as an usher around Park Place Church of God in Anderson, Indiana, he came in contact with everyone, and everyone was a recipient of his heart of gold. Though he was a large man with a dark beard and could look a bit frightening, children loved him. Youngsters would come up to him, grab him around the leg, and ask for a hug. He was very liberal with his hugs and his attention. He could talk about anything with anybody. We were always the last to leave the church on Sunday morning. I would often search for him after the service and find him with the organist, or the pastor, or the janitor, or anyone with whom he wanted to *touch base*. Usually, he wound up doing something during the week for that person either at home or at the church. His charge for doing things for them was a hug. He routinely gave and received them. He loved people, and people loved him.

When his valves gave out and he had a fatal heart attack at age fifty, everyone was in shock. The heart of gold was gone but not forgotten. Suddenly, all those hugs that he had given out over the years came flooding back to me and our son Jordan. The hugs came back to us in biblical proportions–seventy times seven–pressed down, shaken together, and running over. It began on the night of his

Old North Church *(Christ Church)* (1723)
Boston, Massachusetts

*On December 29, 1723, Reverend Timothy Cutler held the
first service. In 1722, King's Chapel had decided to build a
second Anglican church and a site was selected near the
crown of Copp's Hill. It took twenty-three years to complete
the building.*

*On April 18, 1775, Sexton Robert Newman lit two lanterns
in the tower to alert Paul Revere that the British were
arriving by sea which touched off the Revolutionary War.*

death when friends came to our house to clean, cook, and console until early the next morning. Sometimes it was a literal hug; sometimes it came back in the form of food or flowers. Some people made a visit or offered a prayer. Often friends offered to do something I didn't even know needed to be done. Leaves were raked, or dinner invitations were extended. Even weeks later, at the writing of these words, the hugs still come—the letters, the calls, the invitations, the advice, the books, the attention, the arms wrapped around us. Phil's heart of gold hugged everyone. Now, in our time of need, everyone was hugging back.

Philip Michael Slattery
1951-2001

We all have a heart of gold. Probably not a literal one like Phil's, but a heart of gold none the less. How great it is to be a part of a family. How much greater to be a part of the family of God where golden hearts and hugs are in abundance.

"They must keep hold of the deep truths of the faith with a clear conscience."
—1 Timothy 3:9

I've Come This Far...

Sherrill D. Hayes

J have heard persons say, and I have said the same about myself, "I am a child of the church." For me this means the church—the community of faith—has been the most significant influence in the development of my personal faith.

I don't remember going to church or Sunday school before I was five or six years old. It was then that my mother took me around the corner to a little storefront church on Main Street in Ashtabula, Ohio. Because of some difficult family circumstances, which are not especially relevant here, the church—the community of faith—both at that time and ever since has been much like a family to me.
I remember sitting in that storefront church singing:
"One door and only one, and yet its sides are two,
Inside and outside, on which side are you?
One door and only one, and yet its sides are two,
I'm on the inside, on which side are you?"
The theological meanings of that little chorus escaped me.
I thought it was a song about our little church. It had only one door on the street at the front. Since some of my life on the outside of the church was not so good, it was a very good feeling to be *inside the church* where I experienced unusual love and support from persons there.

God has never spoken out loud to me. But God often spoke to me through the people of the church in Ashtabula. It was from them, the Covells, the Boyers, the Bentleys, that I first felt my call to ministry. It was because of their influence that I went to Anderson College in Anderson, Indiana, to study for the ministry. After my first year as a student, I returned home, unable to continue my studies until I had paid my overdue tuition bill. Sister Loomis heard about my dilemma and asked me one Sunday morning how much money I needed in order to go back to college. I told her $180.00, which at that time was a full semester's tuition. On Sunday night, she stopped me in the vestibule and squeezed $180 into my hand.

Trinity United Methodist Church (1797) - *LaGrangeville, New York*

A deed, dated July 24, 1797, describes the plot of land in the Potter's Corners area, Town of Union Vale, which was acquired for the purpose of building the Trinity Methodist Church. It is probable that the building was constructed in or about 1827. Prior to this time, the congregation met in the Beekman Church. The old Dutchess circcuit was established in 1821. In 1832, this circuit consisted of thirteen churches including Trinity Methodist at Union Vale.

In 1862, the church purchased four acres of land at its present site in LaGrangeville for $400. The church at Potter's Corners was taken down in 1863, moved to its present location, and rebuilt. Construction of a community building or parish hall was completed in 1958, and the sanctuary was redecorated to its present state in 1962. In 1976, the church belfry and steeple were restored to their original form.

"I have just one request," she said. I expected her to challenge me to study hard and to serve the Lord faithfully. Instead, she said, "Don't tell Brother Loomis about this." The Bible says, *don't let your left hand know what your right hand is doing.* I thought, now I hear your call, Lord, loud and clear!

Some persons sing, *"I've come this far by faith."* As a retiree, reflecting on how I've gotten this far, I have to say,   I've come this far because of the persons who have believed in me. That brings me to my first pastorate, the First Church of God in Greensburg, Indiana.

So what if you only have finished your junior year of college! When you have been married for three months and are weary of going to classes and working nights in the factory, it's time to move away from all that classroom theory and begin winning the world to Christ. So I thought, when Fritzie, my wife, another whom I had come

Sherrill D. Hayes

to know believed in me, and I drove up to the little white frame church building in Greensburg. We had heard that they had been without a pastor for two years and without worship services for six months. Their search and call process was not complicated.

While walking around the outside of the building we met a neighbor who took us to the home of the treasurer, who introduced us to the chair of the Board of Trustees. I guess someone who had two years of college, and was available, was credentialed enough, so we went home that night having agreed to begin immediately as pastors. Here were more persons who believed in me.

How much I learned during the four years I pastored there:

• How to lift the trap door to the parsonsage cellar to light the hot-water heater whenever you needed hot water.

• How to balance the church budget by selling one of the two outhouses (yes, that kind). With an average worship attendance of eighteen we didn't need two.

• That when the chair of the trustee board said, "Pastor, you need to know that I am an Odd Fellow," it didn't mean what you worried it might mean.

• That if you didn't get your tithe from your second job in the plate on Sunday morning, the treasurer would not be able to give you your $20.00 weekly salary on Sunday night.

• That the best way to start the fire in the stoker-fired furnace on Saturday night was to light corncobs.

• That I wasn't very good at selling Fuller Brushes and the job at the Hub Shoe Store was better.

• But that you should not tell your parishioners that you got a job at the Hub, when *The Hub* was a tavern in the town where the church was located.

Looking back on that pastorate, I wonder how the members of the congregation put up with someone so inexperienced and theologically untrained as I was. I don't have to wonder, however, whether or not they believed in me.

Probably the most significant growth in my faith came from my years in seminary and the Park Place Church of God in Anderson, Indiana. While serving a national agency of the church some years later, we worshipped there. Our children were nurtured there during the first years of their lives. Participating in the life of that church, I came to know and appreciate the value in the diversity of God's children. The community of faith is a community of liberals and conservatives, fundamentalists and modernists, professionals and blue collar workers, diversely and spiritually gifted, but more importantly, brothers and sisters in the family of God. In these communities of faith I have known persons who have believed in me, and because of that I have grown and matured. Thanks be to God!

*"There is one body and one Spirit—just as you were called to one hope
when you were called—one Lord, one faith, one baptism;
one God and Father of all, who is over all and through all and in all."*
—*Epheisans 4:4-6*

Why Not?

Betty Jo Hyman Johnson

When I was twelve, I gave my life to God. At twenty-one I was continuing in my Christian experience, but I really did not think that God had anything out of the ordinary for me.

My parents had moved from Oklahoma to Forest Grove, Oregon, and a few months later I followed them. I had a job as a secretary at an elementary school and I just lived from day to day. I didn't give much thought to what my life-long work would be.

In Forest Grove I had no transportation on Sundays to the closest Church of God in Portland, twenty-five miles away. A little Baptist Church was three blocks away. I started attending there regularly.

One Sunday, a missionary was the preacher. He made an excellent presentation about his work in South America. At the end of his sermon, he challenged all of us to commit our lives to missions. I was deeply moved but thought, "That's not for me." And it was then that what seemed like an audible voice replied, "Why not?" I sat for a few moments and then walked to the altar—I was the only one—and promised God that as He opened the door, I would step through.

I had no idea what lay ahead, but I had said, "Yes, Lord, I answer your call to mission work." I felt such a relief to have some real direction for my life. Within a few months, I was enrolled at Pacific Bible College (now Warner Pacific College) with every intention to do missionary work. I was involved with the Student Volunteer Movement and met my future husband, who was also interested in missions.

We have been involved in missions in one form or another ever since that time. Only one time, and that for only about twenty-four hours, have I ever thought that I had misunderstood God when I heard the question, "Why not?" All of us need to listen to what God is saying to us. How thankful I am that God said to me, "Why not?"

Little Cedar Grove Baptist Church (1812)
Mound Haven, Indiana

Built in 1812, this is the oldest church building still on its original location in the state. In the interior, rifle openings can be seen in the walls, as well as a balcony and raised pulpit. A burial plot adjoins the church.

"They presented these men to the apostles, who prayed and laid their hands on them."
—Acts 6:6

The Church Laid Hold of Me, Then Laid Hands on Me

John A. Howard

I was ordained to the Christian ministry on October 14, 1973. I had long felt the call of God on my life for pastoral ministry, and had prepared myself through college and seminary for that call. On the night of my ordination, it felt that my preparations to answer God's call had come to some fulfillment in my life. It was on later reflection that I realized how much the Church had invested in my preparation. Their faith in God, in His call, and in my being called was the sustaining faith for the journey.

The Certificate of Dedication shows that my parents had me dedicated in June of 1949. The congregation at Southside Church of God in St. Louis, Missouri, was to be my faith home until I left for college in Anderson, Indiana. My earliest teaching about Jesus, my earliest acquaintance with His people came with that family of God. Long before I knew what being a Christian meant, I knew that I was *accepted*. Long before the Church laid hands on me, they laid hold of me and I was accepted as a part of the faith journey.

At a revival meeting in that same church in September, 1957, I gave my heart to the Lord. There was much celebration and even as a child of eight, I knew that something important had happened and would continue to happen in my life. There was a new level of expectation placed on me as I moved into the Christian life. It probably had to do with maturity as well as maturing, but I knew that now the family of God had truly *adopted* me. I was not just one of them, but one with them. They nurtured me, and encouraged me, and chastised me, and worked to bring me to maturity in the faith. Long before the Church laid hands on me, they laid hold of me and I was adopted into the family of God, to join the faith journey.

It was the sixteenth of June, 1963, that I first filled the pulpit. I was

Orange United Methodist Church - *Orange, Indiana*

We were unable to locate any historical information for this church. My father, Sander J. Kleis, pastored the Methodist churches in Glenwood and in Orange from July, 1955, through July, 1956.
The service in Orange was at 8:30 each Sunday morning.
I have fond memories of the peace in that small sanctuary as I sat listening to hymns played on an old upright piano by my mother or a young lady not much older than myself. I remember the golden rays of the early morning sun streaming in through the tall, slender windows and the brilliant blue sky and the flat green fields. It was here that I first remember learning to appreciate my father's use of poetry to close a sermon. I can still remember some of my favorites, Others *and* The Touch of the Master's Hand.

Avis Kleis Liverett

prepared with notes to last a lifetime. Thirteen minutes after I began, I looked over my shoulder to Brother Weaver and said, "Now what do I do?" He helped me out of an awkward time, and encouraged me to begin preparing for the next time I would preach. In spite of what seemed a poor first time, I received nothing but encouragement to continue and training to assist my development, and I did preach again. I was thirteen when I first preached, and to this day I recognize the importance that the church *allowed* me to experience and experiment with what it meant to be called. Long before the Church laid hands on me, they laid hold of me and I was allowed to work as a part of the family of God, to explore the faith journey.

The phone rang on May 13, 1973, and the congregation in Winnipeg, Manitoba, extended an invitation to Nancy and me to come as pastors. With fear, anticipation, excitement, hope and a wide mixture of other emotions, we loaded the U-haul and moved to Winnipeg. Ten years we worked together with those great people, and saw the church move forward. They were a wonderful people to help us develop in our first pastoral experience. At the point of that invitation, and our acceptance to the pastorate in Winnipeg, there was an understanding that the church had *acknowledged* us in the role for which we had prepared. Twenty-nine years of service with the Church of God have followed since then. Still, I know that long before the Church laid hands on me, they laid hold of me and I was acknowledged by being asked to do that for which I had prepared for service within and with the family of God on the faith journey.

I was ordained to the Christian ministry on October 14, 1973. On that night, the Church laid hands on me. I was, in the biblical sense of being "called and sent" *anointed* for that faith journey. But it was because the Church *accepted* me, *adopted* me, *allowed* me, *acknowledged* me and *anointed* me, that I had faith for the journey. *Thank you,* Church!!!

"I do not hide your righteousness in my heart; I speak of your faithfulness and salvation. I do not conceal your love and your truth from the great assembly."
—Psalm 40:10

My Faith Journey

Mary Woods Baker

mall congregations hold a special place in my heart. Why, you might ask. It was in a small congregation in Ypsilanti, Michigan, the Monroe Street Church of God, that I began my walk with the Lord. As I reflect on my spiritual journey, I realize that God has smiled on me for as long as I can remember. I was born to Christian parents, Paul and Mary Woods, and their love for God and the church was nurtured in me. My mother, a schoolteacher by profession, stopped teaching in the public school when her children were born and transferred her gifts in teaching to teaching family values and Christian principles to her children through prayer, family devotions and Bible study.

I was fortunate to be surrounded by many spiritual role models and mentors who significantly influenced my spiritual journey and ministry. Saints like Reverend Thomas Walker, Pastor Jessie Caldwell, Reverend George Marshall, Reverend Roosevelt Williams, Pastor Ralph Offord, Dr. Benjamin Reid and Reverend Libby Wright, who have passed away; as well as Reverend Evelyn Ruth Simpson, Dr. James Earl Massey, Reverend Fred Davis, Reverend Jethro Mosley, Reverend Richard Goode, Reverend Ruby Wideman and Reverend Carolyn Waddy Reid shared words of wisdom and encouragement at just the right time.

At age eleven, Jesus Christ became my Lord and Savior. Later as a teen, I received the call to the Christian ministry. Although life as a teenager brought the usual challenges, somehow God enabled me to remain faithful to my commitment. In October, 1999, I was ordained in the Church of God only after feeling that God was leading me to pursue ordination at that particular time.

God's faithfulness and love have been reaffirmed many times in my life. It was in the most difficult times that I felt closest to God. When news came of my father's death in my sixth month of pregnancy, God's presence gave me comfort and strength. I vividly

Ypsilanti Community Church of God (1925)
Ypsilanti, Michigan

In 1925, Sister Minnie Walker, along with Elder John Richards and Dr. Raymond Jackson, began holding meetings in different homes. As the meetings grew, a tent was erected on First Avenue to hold services. Attendance continued to grow and on August 9, 1931, the first church building on Monroe Street was dedicated.

remember the pain of seeing my brother losing his battle with cancer. Once again, God's presence sustained me.

A few hours after the birth of our second son, our family physician told my husband and me that the nerves in our son's right shoulder were severely damaged in birth and that he would not have the use of his arm on that side. We were told that surgery might correct it. Pastor Ralph Offord came to the hospital, tenderly held our infant son and prayed for him. One month later when a specialist gave us the good news that the X-rays showed no damage at all, I witnessed God's healing power. Years later, my husband and I sat in the bleachers and tears of joy rolled down our cheeks as we proudly watched Stephen play Little League baseball. We thanked God for the joy we knew in that moment.

Theodore means "Gift of God" and I truly believe that my husband is just that. I consider each of our five children–Theodore, Jr., Rebekah Irene, Stephen Carl, Mary Elizabeth and Leah Ann–a precious gift from God. We were blessed to see each child graduate from college and find employment. As I look at my two healthy, vivacious grandsons–Stephen Allen and Aidan Nathaniel–I am reminded once again of the miracle of birth and the awesome God I serve. My simple faith has increased and is sealed by life experiences. My heart with deep sincerity sings with the song poet, "God is *so* good, God is *so* good!"

"For everything created by God is good...If you put these instructons before the brothers and sisters, you will be a good servant of Christ Jesus, nourished on the words of the faith and of the sound teaching that you have followed."
—1 Timothy 4:4, 6

The Church Nurtures Our Faith

Arthur M. Kelly

The church that I grew up in was located on a diamond shaped piece of property on what most considered the wrong side of the tracks. It didn't have an organ—unless you counted the traveling pump organ that Sister Peterson used to bring in on special days and play for us. But it had a steeple, a bell and bell rope. The bell worked and I was allowed to ring it from time to time on Sunday mornings. It was a small clapboard church that looked like it belonged in a New England village rather than in the gritty neighborhood where it was. I doubt that we ever saw one hundred persons in the pews—even during the hottest revivals. But it was big enough for me, cared for me, and formed my faith in important ways. It taught me about Jesus and personally introduced me to Him. It taught me about the church and personally demonstrated it to me. It taught me, not always positively, about the fallenness of persons and showed me how persons who love God are able to rise above their humanity. It was the church but it wasn't the whole church.

I moved to Portland, Oregon, and to college—and the church grew much larger. I attended Holladay Park Church of God, a much larger structure. There was no bell this time, but a split chancel, stained-glass windows, and a powerful Wicks organ. I grew into that church; it was big in many ways. My faith grew in that church; God grew in that church; the church grew in that church. I discovered new music, new thought, new vitality; new horizons; I made my first, real, intelligent commitment to God in that place. Warner Pacific College raised my sights as well—oh my, how it raised my sights! In addition to faculty like Milo Chapman, Irene Smith Caldwell, and Claire Gayle, I heard E. Stanley Jones, missionary to

Spurwink Congregational Church (1802) - *Cape Elizabeth, Maine*

The Spurwink Meeting House was erected in 1802 by the inhabitants of Cape Elizabeth who desired to have their own place of worship. They raised the building themselves on an acre of donated land. The present chandelier was purchased second hand and installed in the late 1800s. Now restored to its original beauty and electrified, it is the focal point of the interior.

The Spurwink Church is the oldest public building in Cape Elizabeth and has been named to the National Register of Historic Places. The handsome steeple and old weathervane continue to be a landmark to residents and visitors. The church's historic character is enhanced by the beauty of the salt marshes it overlooks. Because of its charm the Meeting House is still used by townspeople for weddings, christenings, funerals and other special events.

India; John Crose, missionary to Egypt and the Middle East; Frank Laubach, missionary to the world—oh, the church grew! These two places were the church but they weren't the whole church.

I moved to Red Bluff, California. To a smaller church—no organ, no bell, no stained-glass windows. This is where my children were born and where one died. Out on the edge of town, this church was where my son and daughters were dedicated and where one child was buried. This is where I was baptized—late in life, a little hesitant, but understanding what I was about to do and say. There I found my calling—to be a teacher. There I found my lifelong pastor, Jay Barber, who taught me much about the cost of discipleship and ministry; together we found what many in ministry don't—a comfortable place between pastor and friend. Good people in this church; eager people; salt of the earth people; hard working people who loved God and worked hard at living out their baptism. The church grew! It was the church but it wasn't the whole church.

I moved to Anderson, Indiana, and went to work for Warner Press, the publishing house of the Church of God, the Board of Christian Education, and Church of God Ministries—and to a wonderful place named Park Place Church of God, full of wonderful church folks; the church grew for me, larger and larger. I traveled to Beirut, Lebanon, and found the church there; I traveled to Cairo, Egypt, and found the church there. The international church. The worldwide church. Oh! the church grew and grew; wherever I looked was the church; yes, all of this was the church, but all of this was not the whole church.

In Advent month we celebrate the coming of the Lord of the church, the head of the body; we celebrate the coming of the church, the means by which the rule of God is brought to the whole world. The boundaryless church. The church triumphant—the kingdom of God that exists in the hearts of all persons in whom this Lord dwells. That is the church. The church that comes through persons who take up the disciple's pilgrim life—the church limited only by the willingness of followers to give of themselves, their imaginations, their time, their money, their selves.

I thank the Sovereign Lord of the universe for the idea of the church—and for all of the people and expressions of that idea of the church helping me to grow faithfully as a pilgrim journeying in and through the church toward the kingdom.

"...the boundary lines have fallen for me in pleasant places;...I have a delightful heritage."
—Psalm 16:6

A Wonderful Heritage

Cleda Achor Anderson

I was blessed with a wonderful religious heritage. More than a hundred years ago, my Quaker grandfather, G. R. Achor, gave up a medical career to become a traveling evangelist and missionary, after he was *gloriously saved* in a Church of God tent meeting. My parents met and married when they came to Anderson to join the Gospel Trumpet family in 1906. They were following a similar dream of service, devotion, and commitment. They reared their five children in the very shadow of the Trumpet Home, passing on a wonderful legacy to a third generation.

When I was sixteen, I walked down the center aisle of the old Park Place Church of God to the altar and gave my heart to the Lord. Rooted in such a rich family tradition, I remember feeling "now it is my turn to serve the church." And I did.

I enrolled in Anderson College to take courses that would prepare me for service. A few weeks after my graduation, I was invited to be the first full-time Youth Director of Park Place Church of God. I enjoyed this ministry immensely. I married my high school sweetheart, Joe, and a year later we started our family.

Life became very busy. I jumped full speed into the process of living, working at a still new marriage, running a youth ministries program, and having a baby. Fairly quickly, we were blessed with two more children, and I soon realized the necessity to be a *stay-at-home mom* for a few years.

Ten years went by. My journey of faith, predicated on doing, accomplishing and serving, faltered. I began questioning what I really believed...and why. The legacy of home and church wasn't enough. Somewhere deep within, I felt a call to *be* not just *do*. I sensed a deep, spiritual yearning to be whole, to experience a personal conversion that went beyond family values and more than all my good works.

I sincerely prayed that God would give me the keys to the kingdom; to show me how to experience the rebirth I was seeking. I didn't expect to find it in such a hurtful and traumatic way.

Our family was spending Christmas in Florida with my parents,

Longboat Island Chapel (1956) - *Longboat Key, Florida*

In May, 1956, twenty-five residents of Longboat Key gathered to discuss the spiritual needs of the community. They wished to establish an educational ministry where people could freely express and exchange religious ideas. Thus, Longboat Island Chapel, an interfaith community church was born.

Longboat Island Chapel is a congregation tolerant of divergent religious views that seeks to live at all times in such a state of affection for one another that they are not threatened by differences.

Dr. Cleda Anderson has been associated with and has served on the staff of this faith community for several years.

enjoying the warmth of sun and sand. One morning, our eleven-year-old daughter complained of nausea and headache. She had been bitten by a mosquito and developed encephalitis. The doctors feared she would go into a coma and perhaps die.

My world quickly crumbled apart. I tried praying, but God seemed so far away. I began questioning and blaming Him. After all I had done for His people and His church, was this to be my reward? I admit, I really felt this way. I was going under with fear and grief. Did God even care?

Days went by. I spent hour upon hour walking the beach, wrestling with my need for understanding. Slowly, I felt something changing within. The edges of my fabricated faith started to crumble. I spent a lot of time in solitude, inviting God's grace and Spirit to fill me. It truly was a time of spiritual rebirth and the beginning of deepening insight and pilgrimage that has unfalteringly led me to a vital faith for the rest of my life journey.

In closing, I want to share this poetic reflection I wrote to myself many years ago:

Blessed Crisis

My personal heritage was rich and full,
Indebted to parents I would not trade,
Who gave me a base of values and love.
Thus, my early foundations were laid.

Yet, so narrow and firm my beginnings were,
With family and church so strong,
As they defined my *Who Am I* for me,
How would I think it was wrong?

Not wrong, exactly, but just not enough.
Discovery of me still inside,
To seek personal truth, God's plan for me,
Were awarenesses I no longer could hide.

The years have sped by as the seasons roll,
Some good, some bad, some yet to be trod,
How thankful I am for this journey of faith,
To face life, myself, and my God.

An Emily Dickinson I am not,
And yet I share her thought
That Life without some *deathly blows*
Will surely come to naught!

"...a faith and knowledge resting on the hope of eternal life, which God, who does not lie, promised before the beginning of time,..."
—Titus 1:2

Influence of Grandpa and the County Line Church

Ronald V. Duncan

When I was a boy, it was customary for me to spend some of my summer vacation with relatives "in the country." This journey of about thirty miles was often taken by our family as we visited throughout the year the many aunts, uncles, cousins, and grandparents. I always looked forward to these extended times in the country because I could participate in the farming and logging activities. Obviously, because I was young and inexperienced, I was always under the watchful eye of a senior. When I stayed with the grandparents, they wanted me to work and afforded me the opportunity to learn about farming.

On Sunday morning, however, after the chores were done, Grandpa Heck would put on his best pair of bib overalls and his white shirt in preparation for church. The "County Line Church" was about a quarter mile from the home place. I would walk with Grandpa to the church. He would open the door and then retrieve the rope that rang the bell in the tower. Yes, that was a task I was able to do and he always asked me to ring the bell. The bell would resound throughout the valley telling the neighbors that the door was open and church would start in thirty minutes. The church had a pot-bellied stove up front that Grandpa would start up in the winter time in order to have a cozy building when people arrived. I now know that was one way to get persons to the front pews.

The "County Line Church" was built in 1869 on the county line between Hawkins County and Greene Couny in Tennessee. Couples who were married in the church would stand at the front or rear, depending on the origin of their marriage license. The "County Line Church" has gone through many changes throughout its history, but still stands and serves as a church today to persons in the area.

Providence "County Line Baptist Church" (1869)
Hawkins County & Greene County, Tennessee

*Located exactly on the Hawkins-Greene County line on State
Highway 70, this church is said to be the only church in the
state where the minister stands in one county and the
congregation sits in the other. It is more commonly known as
the "County Line Church" since the county line runs right
through the middle of the church building. If you were
getting married and were from Hawkins County, you were
required to marry at the front door or on the front steps. If
you were from Greene County, you were married at the altar.
According to one of the historians of the church, the first
services of this congregation were held in a barn. One record
says that the early congregation met in a slave cabin. Before
the first church was built, a small log building was erected.*

According to church records that I received recently, my mother was baptized June 3, 1934. Her mother and father, my grandparents, were baptized August 6, 1944. As I read about the history of this country church, I wondered how far-reaching its influence has been and continues to be in the lives of people.

I recall those trips with Grandpa going to ring the bell as very special. Little did I know at that time the road of life that was before me. Yet today, I give thanks for all the persons who have impacted my life. I feel most blessed and I say thanks to all. Let's continue to ring the bells announcing the grace and love of our Lord and Savior, Jesus Christ.

Now Faith Is...

Now Faith is believing
        the promises
                the promises foretold.

Now Faith is receiving
        our lives in trust
                gifts from the Hands of God.

Now Faith is giving
        all that we are
                giving all the living we have.

Faith is the giving
        all of our living
                from our hands
                        to the Hands of God.

And Love is the giving
        all of our living
                from our hearts
                        to the Heart of God...

Christie Smith Stephens

"...whoever wants to become great among you must be your servant,
and whoever wants to be first must be slave of all."
—Mark 10:43-44

The Bath and the Basin

Sharon Olson Collins

ometimes in our faith journeys we have a moment of
epiphany. Something we've heard over and over makes a
new connection to our spirit. One of those times happened
for me when my twin sons were nine or ten months old.

I was a physically and emotionally exhausted new mom. I had
discovered that a tremendous amount of energy had to be expended
to keep these little guys clean, fed, and entertained. No longer did
I have time for myself. So much of what I did each day was tedious.
Often it seemed that no one recognized my efforts. Certainly the
babies weren't giving accolades. Friends didn't really care how many
loads of diapers I washed—or how hard it was to maneuver those
spoons of homemade baby food through grasping little hands into
gaping, spewing mouths. I was used to receiving positive feedback
about the value of my work when I was in the professional world.
But in this new role I was feeling invisible, unappreciated, enslaved.

One day I was bathing the boys and feeling a good deal of self-
pity. Suddenly a memory was evoked by the basin, the splash of the
water, the patting dry of little feet. I remembered the mustiness of
the church basement. A circle of women. Quiet hymns. *"I'll put my
whole heart in his service, and do all he asketh of me..."* The lump of
humility in my throat as someone washed my feet. The satisfaction
I experienced as I washed the feet of another. The warmth in the
embrace between towel-girded parishioners.

I filled with emotion as I thought about Christ's teaching:
*"Whoever wants to become great among you must be your servant, and
whoever wants to be first must be slave of all." –Mark 10:43-44*
Christ did not have to dirty His hands washing the dust from His
disciples' feet. He was not their slave. He was Messiah, King, Lord
of lords. But He chose servanthood. His demonstration of selfless
love cleansed and nurtured His disciples and honored His Father.

My responsibilities with the children were not enslavement, but

First Church of God (1900) - *De Soto, Missouri*

The First Church of God in De Soto began from a distribution of literature by Mrs. Susan Mallicoat. By 1900, three prayer groups were meeting in the De Soto area. James Clemens became the first pastor in the spring of 1910 and the first building was purchased at Blow and East Miller Streets. In 1930, the church moved to a basement structure on Third Street and in 1944 the sanctuary was added.

opportunity. I could choose to humbly serve, both within and beyond our home. I could be a servant leader to my children—a vessel of Christ's love and cleansing and nurture. I could honor God by choosing servanthood.

Bath time became a sacred reminder of Christ's love for me and the blessings bestowed as we serve one another.

Wholehearted Service

Charles W. Naylor, 1874-1950   Andrew L. Byers, 1869-1952

1 I've turned from the world and its fol - lies, For - ev - er for -
2 I will not be lan - guid or care - less, Or for - mal, or
3 Since Je - sus gave all to re - deem me, Since on - ly through
4 O help me, dear Lord, to be read - y The task that thou

sak - en all sin; I've giv - en my - self un - to Je - sus
cold, or un - true; But, striv - ing with ear - nest en - deav - or,
mer - cy I live, It now is my joy and my pur - pose
giv - est to do, Not shrink - ing from la - bor or du - ty,

REFRAIN

To ev - er and on - ly serve him.
The will of my Lord I will do.   I'll put my whole heart in his
A whole-heart-ed serv - ice to give.
De - vot - ed and faith - ful and true.

serv - ice, And do all he ask - eth of me; I mean to live

ho - ly and blame - less— A Chris - tian in - deed will I be.

"So then, those who suffer according to God's will should commit themselves to their faithful Creator and continue to do good."
—1 Peter 4:19

Life's Turning Points

Donald D. Johnson

I look back now, after more than fifty years of service in Christian ministry, and ask, "How did I choose this direction for my life? How is it that kingdom ministry has taken me around the world? What were the deciding factors which formed within me a burning passion for world mission?"

One advantage of being able to look back over one's life is that those spiritual decisions and commitment experiences emerge as clear turning points around which life and ministry is lived out. I can point to two such experiences which are not specific to a moment in time only, but have continued in my spiritual formation and in how I have responded to God's call on my life.

The first took place at the end of my junior year in high school. I was working toward a life in the automobile industry and a job with General Motors. That summer I was confronted by a prominent preacher who took time with me and asked me in all seriousness, "Have you ever considered the ministry?" I honestly felt that God used him to prompt me to listen seriously to what I had already begun to feel but had resisted. Less than a year later, I was off to college to begin preparation for the Christian ministry, a new direction and a lifelong commitment.

The second occurred during my second year at college. I was a member of a group interested in and learning to become world Christians. We were challenged and asked to sign a personal commitment, as we looked ahead to our future ministry in a global context. What I signed in September, 1947, has been my guiding commitment for life. I challenge you to consider it as well:

"I will live my life under God for others rather than for myself. I will not drift through life, but will do my utmost by prayer, by investigation, by meditation and service, to discover that form and place in which I can become the largest use in the Kingdom of God. As I find it, I will follow it under the leadership of Jesus Christ, wheresoever it takes me, cost what it may."

First Congregational Church (1773) - Wiscasset, Maine

This historic church was organized before the American Revolution and has enjoyed a continuous existence. From this site, at the head of the Common, Old First Church has looked out over the village of Wiscasset for over two hundred years. The building in which the congregation now worships is the third erected in this location and was dedicated July 27, 1909.

The second building burned in 1907. Its Paul Revere bell was not completely destroyed and a considerable portion of the metal was cast into the present bell. The weather vane, also made by Paul Revere, was saved and is seen surmounting the present steeple.

"For I know the plans I have for you,...plans to give you hope and a future."
—Jeremiah 29:11

Choosing Faith

Rhonda Rothman Hamm

Faith, to me, means giving up control. Sounds simple, doesn't it? But for most of my life I kept such a tight hold on my neat little world, thinking all the while that I had faith, when all I really had was my idea of control. Life was pretty easy, pretty fun; not a whole lot was required of me. I had all the answers I thought I needed, and was fairly content. Then life started happening: REAL life. And there went my so-called control.

Our first baby threatened my control; in fact he pretty much took over my life. Our second baby, a twenty-five and a half week "micro preemie," who weighed 1 lb. 5 oz. at birth, kept driving the message home: you have no control, you never did, you never will. Control is not an option! But you *can* choose faith.

We had ten months of driving an hour each way to the hospital, dividing our time between our two children. We received so many difficult phone calls from medical personnel that my stomach churned every time the phone rang. There was one phone call in particular...the one where they said our son had coded and we basically needed to come and say goodbye. We stood by his bed that day giving him over and over and over again to God. We chose to have faith that God is in control. He KNOWS the plans He has for us, for a hope and a future regardless of circumstance. It was so incredibly difficult; and I'm sure Mike and I were numb from the shock...but we chose faith, and did our best to relinquish control.

Victor, our precious preemie, is now two, and is about ready to walk independently. We continue to need much faith for the journey. Victor and his brother Bryler are our daily reminders of God's sovereignty. Victor has many struggles, but he faces life with a huge smile and about a dozen dimples for emphasis!

If I were to be completely honest, I'd have to confess that once in a while I long for the good old days when I obliviously thought I was in control. Then I look at my family and see so clearly that God wants so much more for me. He continually gives me faith for the journey, and I choose to embrace it.

Barrs Mill Church of God (1939) - *Sugarcreek, Ohio*

The Barrs Mill Church of God was a Lutheran Church prior to becoming a Church of God in 1939. Many of the Lutheran members stayed with the church after the change. Willis Burrell was president of the original Board of Trustees. Lester Barr, whom the community of Barrs Mill was named after, was the Sunday School treasurer while it was a Lutheran Church. He stayed on in this role for a few years after it became a Church of God.

"I long to dwell in your tent forever and take refuge in the shelter of your wings."
—Psalm 61:4

A Plan for His Church

James D. Lyon

I stood outside, on the broad cement walkway that edged the side of the old brick church building. It was cold; light snow fell quietly, lazily from the sky, backlit by a floodlight as I peered towards heaven.

Monday night, December 17, 1984.

Discouraged and weary, I wept softly, alone. As the young pastor of the congregation that had given me life—the church in which I was raised—I had done everything I knew how to do to appeal to our neighbors to allow the church to expand. The church, which had been worshiping on the same Seattle corner since 1906, faced implacable opposition in the community. I had just been informed by an attorney that our neighborhood would block any attempt the church made to expand; that we were, in fact, not welcome, and that further conversation was useless.

A kind of pastoral Pollyanna, wanting to believe there was a *silver lining* in every cloud, it was hard for me to accept the blanket rejection, the chilling and hostile response to our proposals for the neighborhood's future.

"I don't know what to do, Lord," my heart cried as my lips moved silently, facing the falling snow, staring at the floodlight in the sky. "It's Your church, not mine," I continued, surrendering, at last, every thread of ownership and control.

I loved that corner so much. It was there that my grandfather helped build the church generations ago. It was there I went to vacation Bible school and sat on Sunday mornings listening to my grandmother singing *Heavenly Sunlight*, while wearing an impossible hat. It was there that I met my wife and married her. It was there that I dedicated my children to the Lord. And it was there that I was called to the ministry. I could not comprehend how anyone

Fairview Church of God (1906) - *Seattle, Washington*

The Woodland Park Church of God was outgrowing its accommodations in 1984. The congregation began to plan for expanding. Residents in the communtiy objected to the plans of expansion.

As Pastor Jim Lyon began to look at other options, the old Fairview Elementary School came to mind. The property was available and God prepared the way for the purchase. The Woodland Park Church of God is now the Fairview Church of God.

could not love this church, this place, and not want her to prosper.

"I don't know what to do, Lord." And then, He spoke. Yes, I said: He spoke. God spoke to me. Standing on the cement walkway, next to the old brick church. He spoke clearly, definitively, directly, irrefutably.

His voice was not heard, it was felt. He spoke with words that could be seen, like one sees a memory or knows the answer to a question on a test. They were words that were pressed against my heart, seared into my mind. God said, "Don't worry, Jim, I have bigger things for this church than can ever be accommodated at this site."

As I listened, the heavy weight I carried was suddenly released. I struggled to understand, while at the same time was transformed by joy and warmth and life. Was it the Holy Spirit enveloping me? Was it the freedom of not having to carry "the world upon my shoulders?" Was I breaking down? Or, was I being lifted up? All of these thoughts converged at once. And then I knew. The one God of heaven and earth was reassuring me that He had a plan for His church and that I could trust Him.

The next day, I ran to the church office and began to think outside of *the box*. Within seven days, we signed a letter of intent-to-buy an abandoned school building that had been invisible to us on December 17. Within the year, the Woodland Park Church became the Fairview Church, as it relocated to a new site and moved into a building over four times the size of its old one. Every piece fell into place, perfectly.

"I am the LORD, your Holy One, Israel's Creator, your King.
This is what the LORD says—he who made a way through the sea,
a path through the mighty waters,...Forget the former things;
do not dwell on the past. See, I am doing a new thing!..."
—Isaiah 43:15-16, 18-19

For I Am Going to Do a New Thing

Norma Elmore Brandon

scripture the Lord gave me when we left the pastoral ministry and came to work in the national agencies was Isaiah 43:15-16, 18-19. I claimed the promise *"I am the LORD...who made a way through the sea, a path through the mighty waters...Forget the former things; do not dwell on the past. See, I am doing a new thing!"* As I look back over my life, this has been God's word to me throughout all my years.

My husband, Jerry, and I married at a young age with little money, but a deep faith and love for each other. We had no car, so my father-in-law and fourteen-year-old brother-in-law drove us back to Anderson College in Anderson, Indiana, the next morning after our wedding.

We loaded the car, packing all the wedding gifts and all my belongings in the trunk and in the back seat beside my brother-in-law, Don. There was no room for the chicken coop. It was full of six live chickens my mother-in-law sent for us to live on until my husband got paid. We tied the chickens to the edge of the trunk with the lid open. What a picture for a cartoon, *newlywed hillbillies moving.*

We started out on our honeymoon five hundred miles to Anderson with my father-in-law driving. I was in the middle, Jerry on the other side; Don sat in the backseat among all the gifts. We were making the trip pretty well when it began to rain, then it began to pour and blow. The gifts and clothes were getting soaked, as well as the chickens. We stopped to put the chickens in the back seat with Don. He had been teasing me so much, I thought it served him right to have to crowd in with the chickens. We had to keep the windows rolled up. The smell was indescribable. Believe me, we began to pray, like Noah, for the rain to stop. It made me wonder

Longview Church of God (1911) - *Vinemont, Alabama*

In 1907, the daughter of W. C. Wilhite had a bad toothache and a "Tooth Doctor" was called to remove the tooth. The doctor left a religious tract with Mr. Wilhite. The periodical was called the **Gospel Trumpet**. The Wilhites ordered more literature that they shared with family and friends who gathered together for home prayer meetings.

The meetings grew and in 1911 five men went to the Leeth National Bank in Cullman, Alabama, to borrow the money to build the new church. It was called Union Grove Church of God. Several months later when the note came due, many people were aware of how their lives had been changed and they took up a collection. When the money was counted, there was enough to pay the loan in full. Around 1915, the church became known as "Old Thirteen" because there were only thirteen members attending at the time. Many new families began attending and in 1941, a new building was completed. It is now called Longview Church of God.

what the smell was like on the ark.

Finally, the rain stopped and we were able to put the chickens back in the trunk. We arrived in Anderson ready to begin our new life together. But we had to do something quick with those chickens. Jerry felt it would be no problem. He had watched his mother kill chickens and cut them up all his life. He thought he could wring the chicken's neck like his Mom did, but when he tried it, he let the chicken go, and it stood up and wobbled around with this loose neck. Not having an axe, he used the largest knife we received as a gift and cut its head off. Then he had to pluck the feathers off and take the insides out.

Trying to impress his new bride who was strictly a city girl and found this "new thing" to be almost too much to handle, Jerry was trying to act so in charge and assured, but this quickly ended when he had to stop every few minutes and run for the garbage can to throw up. Needless-to-say, this was a time-consuming event and we spent a memorable first week of our married life getting the chickens into the freezer. We had wonderful chicken dishes that saved money for many weeks and we learned much about each other through this "new experience."

From the very beginning of my life with my minister husband, I learned God would do a new thing. I also learned to embrace the new things, even though many new experiences have been difficult and stretched me beyond what I ever thought I could do. God has been faithful to His Word.

"...According to your faith will it be done to you."
—Matthew 9:29

The Impact of Faith!

David L. Lawson

The church building had been in my little town of 5,000 for many years. It was white stucco with theatre seats. The auditorium could have seated seventy-five, but there were usually far less than that in attendance. The building had been crammed in between the alley and a business and was flanked on the back by a canning factory.

Its basement had two rooms where children could play in the sandbox and where quilting could be done on winter afternoons by the women of the church. Pastors came and went every three or four years. My family was regular in attendance. We sang and prayed and studied God's word. And we grew both physically and spiritually.

That is the church I knew in my childhood. The older ladies often took me aside and whispered, "Surely God has His hand on you! He may well be calling you to ministry!"

They set an example in their faithful response week after week. Sunday school, morning worship, evening worship, midweek prayer service, and any special events such as evangelistic meetings or work sessions found them there! Always there! Always faithful! Always encouraging!

I graduated high school, served in the Army, and returned to marry and settle down as a business person and lay leader in my church. My wife, Paula, and I had first met at the church one evening when her mother was serving as worship leader for a revival campaign. Paula was a vocal music teacher at the elementary and secondary schools and I was employed at the local bank. I was the church treasurer, Sunday school teacher, the youth leader, and a board member.

We were not satisfied. Something was missing! We were committed to the Lord and what we had always known, but it seemed that God was convicting us that something more was needed.

There at the familiar altar where I bowed as a boy to accept my Savior, and returned many times for renewal and forgiveness, we bowed again. This time our decision was for laying aside the safe and secure surroundings, to leave the people and the place where God had been so real, and to prepare through college training for Christian ministry. I knew well my limitations. To consider moving out to full-time Christian service was a reality I had carefully avoided. But it was clear that was the call.

There was no lightning flash or thunderous voice! It was just the very quiet but apparent awareness that my life would never be fulfilled without that call's acceptance.

The little church in Hoopeston, Illinois, that nurtured me,

encouraged me, led me and challenged me, now joyously and faithfully sent me off to do God's will. They gave us, as a farewell gift, a picture of Sallman's head of Christ that still hangs in our bedroom and still reminds us whose we are and whom we serve.

Like the blind men of Matthew 9, my eyes have been opened. Not by the miracle instant touch, but by the faith so freely given me that I might venture out to prepare for and do the work of God. That could not have been had there been no little white stucco church building where the saints gathered and modeled a continuing faith.

They could never have realized what their faith has meant to me. I only now recognize how valuable has been their gift! It's a faith I now embrace as my own and I reflect on years of local, state and national ministry in the Church of God.

First Church of God (1913) - *Hoopeston, Illinois*

The Hoopeston Church of God began in 1913 as a result of a brush-arbor evangelistic meeting held in the pasture of the Beaver farm located in Iroquois near Wellington. The church met in various homes and then used a building on Main Street.

In the 1920s a small church building was erected at the corner of East Penn and First Avenue. This building was used in the 1930s under the pastorates of Wesley Harrington, Walter Rawlings, Henry Stamm, Walter Evans and others. J. F. Selvidge was pastoring when a new building was dedicated in 1967.

"Enlarge the place of your tent, stretch your tent curtains wide, do not hold back..."
—Isaiah 54:2

Enlarge the Site of Your Tent

Juanita Evans Leonard

On New Year's Eve, 1959, in a small church in Hoopeston, Illinois, God spoke to me through the pages of Isaiah 54, *"Sing, O barren woman, you who never bore a child..."* The tears began to flow from my nineteen-year-old eyes. I knew that there was a message in this scripture for me. Was it telling me that I would not marry? Was I to live as a single woman? After the service, I dismissed the scripture and started back to Anderson College in Indiana.

Springtime brought with it a wonderful relationship with my future husband. We married in June, 1961. On our first anniversary, Samuel complained of pain in his leg and began treatment for bone cancer. By April, 1963, Samuel went to be with the Lord. During that time, so many people cared for both of us through prayer, bringing meals, doing our laundry, and just loving us.

About a week after his memorial service, Isaiah 54 came to my heart again with new meaning. Verses 2 and 3 gave me a new vision and hope for going on with the ministry that God had called me to when I was fifteen: *"Enlarge the place of your tent, stretch your tent curtains wide, do not hold back...your descendants will dispossess nations..."*

Lawrence Samuel Leonard and I had planned to go to Mexico as missionaries. The road to the mission field changed with Samuel's passing, but I continued to follow the call. Sam was encouraging even up to the moment before his death. Through all of the months of radiation, the removal of his leg, and physical therapy, he had encouraged me to continue with graduate studies. He saw my preparation as an insurance policy for the future.

Throughout the years, it has been my privilege to minister on several continents, teaching students from various cultures. They truly have been the ones who have "enlarged the site of my tent" and have allowed me to "stretch out" beyond anything that I could have imagined. God has allowed me to see my "descendants" work in the cities and towns of the world!

Greenbush United Methodist Church (1898)
Greenbush Township, Clinton County, Michigan

Greenbush United Methodist Church began meeting over one hundrd and fifty years ago. They held services in grange halls, homes, and maybe even in a barn or two. Finally the current structure was raised and dedicated to the glory of God for the public meeting and worship of the Greenbush Methodist Episcopal Congregation in 1898.

Since then, many dedicated Christians have raised families, worshiped, married, been buried and found the Lord within its wooden walls and stained-glass windows. Many remember the church being bigger when they were little, warm and cheery in winter, and a bit hot in the dog days of summer. Yet when they and their families return it feels like coming home.

"'But LORD,' Gideon asked, 'how can I save Israel? My clan is the weakest in Manasseh, and I am the least in my family.' The LORD answered, 'I will be with you.'"
—Judges 6:15-16

Meanderings

Jim B. Luttrell

The faith journey is different for each of us, depending upon our focus. Mother Teresa said, "Faith keeps the person that keeps the faith." What that says to me is that a clear focus will result in diminished frustration and disappointment. Sometimes our life situation may seem to make it impossible for us to make any meaningful progress. But it is our inner fears, which evoke hopelessness and despair. Someone said, "It's not the work of life, but the worry of life that robs us of strength and breaks down our faith." Life is full of circumstances that can cause us to worry. But there are some situations that compound our ability to forego worry. Things like unresolved conflicts, unrealized dreams, unhappy relationships, unfulfilled aspirations are examples. How we look at, deal with, and resolve these situations of life determines our ability to move on and to be productive in our life pursuits. John Maxwell said, "...Where there is hope for the future there is power for the present." Hope is a provider of fuel for the tasks of the journey.

Mistakes. We all make them, and we must accept them as a part of life's journey. The one who has never made a mistake is mistaken! Some of the negative challenges along my faith journey ironically served to help me grow and produce more positive results.

I experienced the gift of grace after walking out of a final exam; I grew in my individual areas of ministry as I plodded through a difficult staff ministry situation; I learned to apply grace to myself when I had to leave a place without accomplishing fully all of the things that I had hoped to accomplish; and I learned about the frustrations of single parenting and developed closer relationships with my daughters, following the death of my wife. Thus, with the challenges to our faith can also come fulfillment and rewards.

Other fulfillments along the path include the satisfaction of having

Community Chapel Church of God (1925) – *Lanett, Alabama*

In 1925, Posey Holladay moved to Lanett and his children attended several different Sunday schools in local churches. Soon after, Holladay was out walking and he became conscious of a decision that God wanted him to make regarding having a Sunday school class for his children in his own home. He had become acquainted with the publication known as the Gospel Trumpet *during a ten weeks for ten cents campaign when Mrs. Fannie Clark issued him a subscription. He decided to order Sunday school materials from the Church of God publishing house and began a Sunday school in his home. Soon his home was filled with people studying the lessons.*

a part in the laying of foundations for a broadened ministry base of a given congregation; the expansion of ministry areas such as the development of small group ministry and discipleship ministry. Also, having the opportunity to develop a blended family, and seeing them grow into responsible and responsive young adults who have now yielded four wonderful grandchildren.

I would like to share a few meanderings which might be helpful to some in the faith journey. Seek out people to be around who are encouragers. Invest yourself in a cause that is worthwhile and in people who are positive. Believe in results. God can do anything; it is we who limit the scope of our own efforts. Live daily. Plan, yes, but don't try to anticipate what may happen if.... Remember that God's love is free. We can't earn it by trying to do more and more in order to please Him or earn His favor. He just loves us! Accept it and bask in His goodness. Remember also, that what God calls us to do, He also equips us to do.

Believing in one's self is the beginning of self-actualization. A sense of humor is a spiritual gift. Laughter from the soul releases good endorphins, healthy hormones secreted by the brain, which produce good physical health. Thus, the ability to laugh produces good mental health, *even if it means laughing at yourself.* Leave your comfort zone occasionally. We need new stimulation and taking risks is an act of faith.

Gideon was taken by his own weakness. He asked, *"...how can I save Israel? My clan is the weakest in Manasseh, and I am the least in my family.'" –Judges 6:15.* And yet, when the spirit of God came upon him, he became one of the greatest leaders in the Old Testament.

Finding meaning in life is the key to living it successfully. What gives life meaning? Not things, not power, not money, not position, not the biggest church. Then what? What gives life meaning is to have a purpose, a reason to get up every day, to know who you are, to be guided by principle and to be motivated and filled with Agape love.

An unknown author said, "Do not follow where the path may lead. Follow God where there is no path and leave a trail." That's faith in action.

Robert Louis Stevenson wrote, "Don't judge each day by the harvest you reap but by the seeds you sow."

The faith journey is a seed-sowing journey.

"See, I am doing a new thing! Now it springs up; do you not perceive it?
I am making a way in the desert and streams in the wasteland."
—Isaiah 43:19

Wilderness

Christie Smith Stephens

The summer of 2000 my dad, B. R. Smith, our friends, Mike and Carol Coleman, my husband Stan and I went to Alaska. It was a vacation, a journey and a pilgrimage. Thoreau says, "We need the tonic of wilderness." Belden Lane tells us, "Fierce landscapes serve as metaphorical maps of the life of the spirit" and that "the wildest most dangerous trails are always the ones within." I have found it so. I have found it so.

Alaska

I must more than remember you.
I am compelled to claim you
if not as spiritual home
as does the small strong
Park Ranger woman
who has lived twenty years
in tiny Gustavus perched
on the eastern entrance to
Glacier Bay, claim you as
spiritual haven, spiritual harbor
on my journey of life, of faith.
Spiritual harbor, haven I can
visit when my too little world
envelops me, crowds my soul.

Alaska
I must more than remember
your large stunning white
haired peaks rising above
your rhythmic eternal waters,

St. Michael's Russian Orthodox Cathedral (1848) - *Sitka, Alaska*

In 1848, the Cathedral of St. Michael's was built and became the seat of Bishop Kamchatka, the Kurile and Aleutian Islands, and Alaska. In 1867, the sale of Alaska to the United States ended this "Golden Age" of the Orthodox Church. The priests and monks who served the Church in Alaska overcame many obstacles. They contended daily with bitter cold and deep snows, traveling by dogsled to attend their widely dispersed parishes.

The constant lack of resources led them to sell candles and books, and to sometimes sacrifice their own salaries to meet parish expenses. Despite the sale of Alaska to the United States, the Russian Orthodox priests continued their mission, leaving an indelible mark upon the culture of the Native Alaskans, visible even today.

your ice blue glaciers crashing
the silence, your fireweed spreading
across a ground of cold being.
I must more than remember
your whales breaching, waving
to the stranger, your eagles
sitting for hours atop Sitka
spruce trees then soaring
and swooping to take a ride
on an iceberg, your petroglyphs
revealing messages from the
very first nations, your sea otters
doing the backstroke making
me smile.

Alaska
I need to more than remember you,
your wilderness, your wildness
rushing my mind, enlarging
my vision, refreshing my spirit.
I need to sail my little canoe
on your seafoam green glacial
waters, see your lights flashing
across the dark sea, anchor in
your ports receiving rough garnets
mined by the children. I need to
climb your steep paths, rest by
your crystal waterfalls, breathe
in the violets and heather
blooming in the mountain meadows.
I need to be led by the still waters
of Lake Bennett.

Alaska
I need to more than remember you.
I need to stand with your totems,
your great world trees reaching
between worlds, to learn to read
the stories carved here, to understand
the shaman who cut his hair, put on

shoes to avoid the missionaries' jail.
I need to see St. Michael the Archangel
saved from the sea now witnessing
in your redeemed from the fire
Russian Orthodox Cathedral
just down the road from the
Raptor Center where injured birds
are healed, returned to flight.

Alaska
I sit at the top of your holy mountain.
I claim the power of your creatures.
Raven brings me the sun. I ride on
Thunderbird's wings through your
blue cloud skies. Three frogs are lifted
in honor of my foolishness and shame.
Like the salmon I smell something
in the water that shows me the
upstream way home.

Alaska
Golden journey renewing my mind,
increasing my wonder,
expanding the frontiers of my faith,
wild tonic, dangerous labyrinth,
rising from your Resurrection Bay
I set the albatross free.

Alaska
I shall more than remember you.
I will, Forget-you-not.

"He restores my soul."
—Psalm 23:3

Lessons of Life

Jeannette Crites Flynn

The lessons of life from God come at the most unexpected times and are unmistakably clear. As senior pastor of a large and growing church, I was absorbed with the duties, responsibilities and dynamics of leading, preaching, and discipling. As a working wife and mother of a high school student and a college student, I was constantly trying to balance the hours of my day and meet everyone's expectations! Doing *the right thing* well had been a strong part of my early training. While I valued that heritage, it had also helped produce guilt and a sense of failure as familiar companions in my life. Life was becoming a treadmill of duties, responsibilities and obligations.

Thursday morning dawned. I headed off to the office. I looked through the day's agenda of appointments and meetings and reviewed the list of letters to write, phone calls to make and other normal office duties to handle. I began looking for ways to make some shifts, ease the requirements of the day and get everything done.

My secretary came to the door. "Pastor, Dorothy is here. She'd like to see you." Dear, sweet Dorothy. Seven years earlier she had been traveling by Amtrak to visit family back east. There was a horrendous crash. Several lives were lost, many injured. When Dorothy finally became conscious, she found herself in an unfamiliar hospital in a distant state. Everything seemed fuzzy and jumbled together. The tests and examinations revealed that Dorothy had suffered serious brain damage during the accident. As life unfolded, this once capable, gifted, woman was left with the limited abilities of a ten to twelve-year-old. After a little over a year her husband left her, unable to bear the pain or responsibility any longer. Her teenage sons moved out and on with their lives, not sure how to relate to this person who was once their caregiver and now required more care than they could give. Dorothy was confused and hurt by all of these matters, and yet there was also a childlike innocence that kept her upbeat and positive.

United Church of Fayetteville
American Baptist Presbyterian
(1917) - *Fayetteville, New York*

In 1792, a Baptist lay leader began conducting meetings for prayer and meditation in homes. A meeting house was constructed in 1830. The Presbyterians who had been worshiping in a home, built the first church in town in 1829. Both congregations went their separate ways until 1917. Due to a coal shortage it was agreed to hold joint services. In 1933, the United Church of Fayetteville was established. The Baptist Church building was sold and razed and the present facility became the home of the United Church. A fellowship hall and church school addition was completed in 1953. In 1992, renovations included sanctuary restoration, steeple preservation and other improvements. For this community the United Church has become a beacon and focal point.

She lived three or four blocks from the church and had developed a pattern of dropping by whenever the mood struck. Usually, I didn't mind at all. She never stayed too long. She generally just wanted to tell me what she was up to or what was bothering her. But today really wasn't a good time! "See if you can talk to her today," I suggested. Within two minutes, my secretary reappeared. Shaking her head gently she stated, "She wants to see you." "Okay, send her in," I relented.

Dorothy came through the door grinning. The first words out of her mouth were, "I love you, Pastor Flynn." "I love you too, Dorothy," I acknowledged and genuinely meant it, even though I was wishing that we could share this conversation another time. Dorothy launched into a list of all the reasons why she loved me and why she thought I was the best pastor she had ever known. Not only was this highly unusual for Dorothy, it was a bit uncomfortable for me since I knew all too well my list of short-comings, including the fact that just a few moments ago I had tried to avoid this meeting.

I tried to change the subject, asked about her, thanked her politely, but she was on a mission. She continued to tell me all the things she thought everyone appreciated about me until finally I said, "Dorothy, you have me on a very high pedestal. That's dangerous." She looked at me genuinely puzzled. "I can't live up to all those expectations, I might disappoint you," I explained, being more honest with Dorothy than I would have with anyone else. "Then I would fall off that pedestal and get hurt," I concluded. Her eyes lit up, the smile spread across her face again, she spread out her arms in an open circle and with a focused gaze she responded, "No you won't, 'cause if you fall, we'll just catch you and hug you and help you back up." My tears flowed without embarrassment. The minister in that room that day was Dorothy, not I.

I needed that Divine lesson. She reminded me that the love of God for me is not based on how many things I do, or how well I do them, or even if I get it all right. He doesn't have a list of expectations that when I meet them He is pleased with me and if I don't He is disappointed. She reminded me that God's response to our failures is to catch us in His arms, hug us and help us back up. Dorothy was the living witness of what the body of Christ is really meant to be.

I've failed to meet the expectations of myself and others every-so-often since that day. They haven't always responded the way Dorothy did and I still feel guilt and failure more often than I'd like when I don't accomplish all that is set before me. But God keeps using the lesson Dorothy taught to remind me that His love for us is generous and good. We are His good pleasure and the apple of His eye. His arms are ready to restore even those of us who know Him best.

Psalm 23

A psalm of David.

The LORD is my shepherd, I shall not be in want.
He makes me lie down in green pastures,
he leads me beside quiet waters,
he restores my soul.
He guides me in paths of righteousness
for his name's sake.
Even though I walk
through the valley of the shadow of death,
I will fear no evil,
for you are with me,
your rod and your staff,
they comfort me.

You prepare a table before me
in the presence of my enemies.
You anoint my head with oil;
my cup overflows.
Surely goodness and love will follow me
all the days of my life,
and I will dwell in the house of the LORD
forever.

"We live by faith, not by sight."
—2 Corinthians 5:7

Faith—
a Gift to Us All

Lolly Bargerstock-Oyler

Several years ago while in the midst of conversation, a friend looked down at my swollen, pregnant belly and softly said, "Your faith is a gift to us all." The power and sincerity with which she spoke proved overwhelming to me. Politely thanking her, I hurried out of the restaurant where we had been dining, narrowly making it to the safety of my car before deep sobs erupted.

Her statement was a reference to my having had cancer surgery just one year prior to becoming pregnant. When my husband and I had decided to have another child, I viewed our choice as an act of moving forward in life. My friend viewed it as an act of faith. She was not aware of the intense spiritual struggle that had plagued me after the diagnosis. Those who loved me had offered up comforting scriptures and holy revelations that had guided them in times of great distress. Many nights, I lay awake reciting these passages until they became as bland and unremarkable as numbered sheep jumping over fences. Fear ruled my heart and peace was elusive. Eventually I moved out of that melancholy place, but I had come to see myself as relatively faithless.

Now months later, this woman's words had traveled to a tender spot within, offering salvation from my self-doubt. I wept because I believed her to be right. Choosing to have another child was an act of faith. And while we often speak of faith in mystical, David and Goliath type imagery, we most often choose faith in quiet, simple ways. So it is with each day. We rise to the mundane and extraordinary events of life, silently claiming faith. Faith that some good will inhabit the day. Faith that we will discover purpose in our being. And faith that we are loved beyond reason, even in our most human moments. This faith is a gift to us all.

United Brethren Church (1882)
Miami County, Wawpecong, Indiana

The United Brethren Church in Wawpecong was organized by Thomas Evans in 1882. The church was a part of the Converse Circuit of the Whitewater Conference of the United Brethren Church. Charter members included Catharine Troyer, William H. Kling, Dr. D. C. Maughmer, Margaret Maughmer, Matthew Anaker, Margaret Anaker, Mrs. D. R. Smith, Henry Migrants, Nancy Migrants, Frank Migrants and Joseph Migrants. The church has been closed since 1968.

Contributing Writers

Christina Tellechea Accornero lives in Anderson, Indiana. Dr. Accornero is currently serving the eccumenical church community as the Managing Partner of Bethany House Ministries, a multifaceted, ecumenical, renewal and restoration ministry. *(see page 117)*

Cleda Achor Anderson and her husband Joe live in Holmes Beach, Florida. Dr. Anderson is a former Associate Pastor of Longboat Island Chapel. She was the first Youth Pastor at Park Place Church of God and former Dean of Students at Anderson University in Anderson, Indiana. *(see page 253)*

James A. Albrecht and his wife Betty live in Anderson, Indiana. Jim served in the Middle East and Eastern Europe twenty-one years and helped launch a new church in Russia. He currently writes missions, devotional and curriculum articles for Church of God publications and leads missions-study groups aboard. *(see page 129)*

John L. Albright and his wife Ruth live in Sterling Heights, Michigan. John is Senior Pastor of Bethany Church of God near Detroit. He was Youth Director for the National Board of Christian Education of the Church of God. *(see page 188)*

Mary Woods Baker and her husband Ted live in Anderson, Indiana. Mary recently retired from WOMEN OF THE CHURCH OF GOD as Program Coordinator. She has written for *Pathways* and was editor of *Connection* newsletter. *(see page 247)*

Ilene Gray Bargerstock and her husband Rod live in Anderson, Indiana. Ilene has been a pastor's wife and retired as office manager from Church and Ministry Service of the Church of God. *(see page 182)*

Lolly Bargerstock-Oyler and her husband Tim live in Anderson, Indiana. Lolly is a licensed clinical social worker currently employed in home health care. She serves as a social work adjunct faculty member for Anderson University. *(see page 288)*

Cheryl Johnson Barton and her husband Bernie live in Tokyo, Japan. She is a writer and a missionary. *(see page 191)*

James W. Bradley and his wife Judy live in Ocala, Florida. Dr. Bradley is on the faculty at Warner Southern College. Formerly he was the Director of Pastoral Studies at Anderson University School of Theology in Anderson, Indiana. *(see page 99)*

Judy Craig Bradley and her husband Jim live in Ocala, Florida. Judy was office manager for Church of God World Service in Anderson, Indiana. *(see page 166)*

Norma Elmore Brandon and her husband Jerry live in Anderson, Indiana. Norma has worked at the Board of Church Extension, Anderson University School of Theology and CBH/Mass Media of Church of God Ministries. Although retired, she continues as a CBH consultant and CBH Montreat conference host. *(see page 269)*

Christy Spaulding Boyer and her husband Mark live in Anderson, Indiana. Christy is an artist and a writer. *(see page 132)*

Kathleen Davey Buehler and her husband Keith live in Anderson, Indiana. Kathleen is Children's Editor of *Bridges Curriculum* for the Church of God. She is also the author of seven books. *(see page 78)*

Dondeena Fleenor Caldwell and her husband Maurice live in Anderson, Indiana. Dondeena and her husband were career missionaries in Mexico and Brazil. She was editor of *Church of God MISSIONS* magazine for sixteen years and currently writes a weekly column for the *Anderson Herald Bulletin. (see page 230)*

Barry L. Callen and his wife Arlene live in Anderson, Indiana. Dr. Callen is University Professor of Christian Studies at Anderson University and Editor of Anderson University Press. He has authored twenty-four books. He is also a former Dean of both Anderson University and Anderson University School of Theology. *(see page 151)*

Samuel D. Collins and his wife Sharon live in Anderson, Indiana. Sam is currently a Staff Writer for Church of God Ministries. *(see page 198)*

Sharon Olson Collins and her husband Sam live in Anderson, Indiana. Sharon is a Professor of Social Work at Anderson University in Anderson, Indiana, where she directs the Social Work Program. She has served as chair of the Peace and Conflict Transformation Program at the university. *(see page 259)*

David L. Coolidge and his wife Shirley live in Anderson, Indiana. David is Minister of Worship and Arts Emeritus at Park Place Church of God. *(see page 169)*

Kenneth E. Crouch and his wife Carolyn live in Muncie, Indiana. Ken is Senior Minister at Eden United Church of Christ and a former staff member in the Admissions Office at Anderson University in Anderson, Indiana. *(see page 90)*

Ronald V. Duncan and his wife Martha live in Anderson, Indiana. Dr. Duncan has pastored in Ohio, Indiana and Texas. He is the General Director of Church of God Ministries and is a chaplain in the National Guard with the rank of Major. *(see page 256)*

James L. Edwards and his wife Deanna live in Anderson, Indiana. Dr. Edwards is the fourth president of Anderson University. He has pastored in Indiana, Michigan and Ohio. *(see page 126)*

Robert E. Edwards and his wife Jan live in Kandern, Germany. Bob has been a missionary all of his working life. For twenty-eight years he has served and ministered in Tanzania and Kenya. Currently he works in Europe, CIS and the Middle East for Outreach Ministires of the Church of God. *(see page 211)*

Annalou Deese Espey lives in Anderson, Indiana. Lucy and her late husband Joe pastored churches in Indiana and Florida. She is a retired teacher. *(see page 223)*

William E. Ferguson and his wife Debbie live in Takoma Park, Maryland. Bill is Senior Pastor of National Memorial Church of God in Washington, D.C. *(see page 220)*

Jeannette Crites Flynn and her husband Charles live in Anderson, Indiana. Jeannette has pastored churches in Indiana and Washington. She has served as Director of Church and Ministry Service of the Church of God and presently is the Director of the Congregational Ministries Team for Church of God Ministries. *(see page 284)*

Gloria Sickal Gaither and her husband Bill live in Alexandria, Indiana. Dr. Gaither is a writer, songwriter and speaker. She has authored many books and has written lyrics for more than six hundred songs. With the Gaither Trio she has also recorded over sixty albums. *(see page 48)*

Walter R. Gatton and his wife Eileen live in Port Orange, Florida, near Daytona Beach. Walter has pastored in Ohio, Michigan and West Virginia. He serves as Associate in Pastoral Care at the White Chapel Church of God in South Daytona, Florida. *(see page 120)*

Wayne R. Gordon and his wife Patsy live in Anderson, Indiana. He is the National Director of Government Relations of CAT-ASI. *(see page 217)*

Dwight L. Grubbs and his wife Sylvia live in Anderson, Indiana. Dr. Grubbs is a former Professor of Applied Theology at Anderson University School of Theology. He has pastored in Louisana, Texas and Indiana. *(see page 138)*

Jerry C. Grubbs and his wife Jan live in Anderson, Indiana. Dr. Grubbs retired as Dean of Chapel at Anderson University. He also served as Vice-President for Student Life and Dean of Anderson University School of Theology. *(see page 226)*

Sylvia Kennedy Grubbs and her husband Dwight live in Anderson, Indiana. Sylvia is a watercolor artist and is an Associate Minister at Park Place Church of God. *(see page 214)*

Arlene Stevens Hall and her husband Kenneth live in Anderson, Indiana. Arlene is the author of several books on Christian Education and is Minister of Christian Education Emerita at Park Place Church of God. *(see page 102)*

Kenneth F. Hall and his wife Arlene live in Anderson, Indiana. Dr. Hall is the author of several books and was Editor of Curriculum at Warner Press and a former Professor of Christian Education at Anderson University. *(see page 72)*

Ronald O. Hall and his wife Maxine live in Hartselle, Alabama. He retired as an engineer from the space industry in Huntsville, Alabama. *(see page 194)*

Rhonda Rothman Hamm and her husband Mike live in Anderson, Indiana. She is a former middle school teacher who has presently chosen to stay home with her two sons. *(see page 264)*

Daniel C. Harman and his wife Betty live in Anderson, Indiana. Dan is the author of four books. He also served nine years as an editor with Warner Press. (see page 59)

Sherrill D. Hayes and his wife Phyllis live in Lake Wales, Florida. Dr. Hayes is the former Executive Secretary of the National Board of Christian Education of the Church of God. He is now teaching at Warner Southern College. (see page 238)

John A. Howard and his wife Nancy live in Camrose, Alberta, Canada. John is the Chief Operations Officer and Dean of Faculty at Gardner College. (see page 244)

Betty Jo Hyman Johnson and her husband Don live in Anderson, Indiana. Betty Jo is a former missionary in Trinidad and Guyana and a pastor's wife. She was an elementary school teacher. (see page 242)

Donald D. Johnson and his wife Betty Jo live in Anderson, Indiana. Dr. Johnson is the former Executive Director of the Missionary Board of the Church of God. He was a missionary in Trinidad and Guyana and is Senior Pastor Emeritus at Park Place Church of God. (see page 262)

Don Deena Johnson lives in Anderson, Indiana. Don Deena was the principal of the Fairview Christian School in Seattle, Washington, and has taught at Tamagawa Seigakuin School in Tokyo, Japan. Recently she was on the faculty at Mediterranean Bible College in Beruit, Lebanon. (see page 124)

John M. Johnson and his wife Gwen live in Beruit, Lebanon. John is President of Mediterranean Bible College and pastor of Beirut International Church. He has been a missionary in Korea, Egypt and Lebanon. (see page 111)

Arthur M. Kelly and his wife Judy live in Anderson, Indiana. Arthur is the Coordinator of Publications for Church of God Ministries. He was formerly the Dean at Warner Pacific College in Portland, Oregon. (see pages 33 and 250)

Philip L. Kinley and his wife Phyllis live in Anderson, Indiana. Dr. Kinley was a missionary in Japan serving from 1955 until 1998 as a pastor, church planter and school administrator. (see page 172)

Phyllis Gillespie Kinley and her husband Philip are retired and live in Anderson, Indiana. They served as missionaries in Japan for forty-three years. (see page 175)

Dale D. Landis and his wife Bonnie live in Pendleton, Indiana. He is Minister of Music at South Meridian Church of God in Anderson, Indiana. (see page 160)

David L. Lawson and his wife Paula live in Anderson, Indiana. Dr. Lawson is a former Director of World Service for the Church of God. (see page 272)

Juanita Evans Leonard lives in Anderson, Indiana. Dr. Leonard is an Associate Professor at Anderson University School of Theology and is a licensed Marriage and Family Therapist. Juanita is a widely published author. (see page 275)

James L. Lewis and his wife Barbara live in Anderson, Indiana. Dr. Lewis has pastored in North Carolina. James is Associate Professor of Christian Ethics at Anderson University in Anderson, Indiana. He has authored the book, *Stewardship: Whole Life Discipleship. (see page 145)*

Avis Kleis Liverett and her husband David live in Anderson, Indiana. Avis was an elementary teacher both in Marion, Indiana, and in Anderson, Indiana. She works as office manager for D. Liverett Graphics. *(see page 20)*

Jim B. Luttrell and his wife Wendy live in Lanett, Alabama. Jim is Pastor of the Community Chapel Church of God in Lanett. He has pastored churches in Indiana, Ohio, Tennessee and Michigan. *(see page 277)*

James D. Lyon and his wife Maureen live in Anderson, Indiana. Dr. Lyon is Senior Pastor of North Anderson Church of God and Speaker for ViewPoint, CBH-English radio broadcast for Mass Media, Church of God Ministries. He was Senior Pastor of Fairview Church of God in Seattle, Washington, and a member of the Washington State House of Representatives. *(see page 266)*

David E. Markle and his wife Peggy live in Anderson, Indiana. Dr. Markle taught in the Bible and Religion Department at Warner Pacific College in Portland, Oregon, before coming to Park Place Church of God as Senior Minister. *(see page 203)*

James Earl Massey and his wife Gwendolyn live in Greensboro, Alabama. Dr. Massey is the author of several books. He was Dean of Chapel at Tuskegee University and served as Campus Minister at Anderson University and Dean of the Anderson University School of Theology. He is also a former speaker for the Christian Brotherhood Hour. *(see page 62)*

Joy L. May lives in Anderson, Indiana. Joy was a journalism major at Anderson University in Anderson, Indiana. She is the Senior Writer for Anderson University and does freelance editing for Thomas Nelson Publishers and Warner Press. *(see page 92)*

T. Franklin Miller and his wife Gertie live in Anderson, Indiana. Dr. Miller was Executive Secretary of the Board of Christian Education of the Church of God and President of Warner Press. He is the author of several books. *(see page 17)*

Charles N. Moore and his wife Elizabeth live in Clearwater, Florida. He has pastored churches in Tennessee, Alabama, California and Ohio. *(see page 142)*

John A. Morrison (1893-1965) was the first president of Anderson College, now Anderson University. Dr. Morrison authored several books. *(see page 232)*

Eugene W. Newberry and his wife Agnes live in Anderson, Indiana. Dr. Newberry is a former Dean of Anderson University School of Theology. Dr. Newberry has authored four books. *(see page 28)*

Arlo F. Newell and his wife Helen live in Anderson, Indiana. Dr. Newell is a former Editor-in-Chief of Warner Press. He is the author of five books and has pastored in Indiana, North Carolina, Missouri and Ohio. *(see page 75)*

Helen Jones Newell and her husband Arlo live in Anderson, Indiana. Helen has taught in the Bible and Religion Department at Anderson University and has written adult curriculum for Warner Press. *(see page 108)*

Robert A. Nicholson and his wife Dorothy live in Anderson, Indiana. Dr. Nicholson is a former Dean of Anderson University and was the university's third President. He was the founder of the Anderson College Choir. *(see page 122)*

Richard H. Petersen and his wife Barbara live in Scarborough, Maine. Dr. Petersen, now retired, was the founding senior pastor of Christchurch of Portland, Maine. He was the Executive Director of the Bible Society of Maine, working in co-operation with the International and American Bible Societies. *(see page 66)*

Harold L. Phillips lives in Anderson, Indiana. Dr. Phillips is a former Editor-in-Chief of Warner Press and was a Bible Professor at Anderson University School of Theology. He has authored several books. *(see page 114)*

Hollis S. Pistole and his wife Elizabeth live in Anderson, Indiana. Dr. Pistole was Professor of Homiletics at Anderson University School of Theology. He has pastored congregations in Ohio and Maryland. *(see page 83)*

Dondeena Bradley Ramey and her husband Allen live in New York City. Dr. Ramey is a Principal for the Health Business Partners Consulting practice with a broad experience in shaping health-based ideas into relevant business propositions. She speaks at industry conferences and is published on a variety of topics relevant to nutrition and health science. *(see page 56)*

Geraldine Hurst Reardon (1919-2001) was First Lady of Anderson University while her husband, Robert H. Reardon, was president for twenty-five years. Dr. Reardon was a high school English teacher in Anderson, Indiana. At the early age of thirteen she began speaking to youth groups and soon was holding evangelistic meetings across the country. She was ordained at the age of eighteen. *(see page 157)*

Robert H. Reardon lives in Anderson, Indiana. Dr. Reardon was the second President of Anderson College, now Anderson University. He has authored several books. *(see page 14)*

Herschell D. Rice lives in Pomona, California. Dr. Rice has pastored in Indiana, Kentucky and California. He was chairperson of the publication board at Warner Press for twenty-four years and has preached in fifty countries. *(see page 24)*

W. Malcolm Rigel and his wife Martha live in Lake Wales, Florida. Dr. Rigel has been a pastor, songwriter, church planter/builder, counselor and professor at two colleges and a seminary. In his retirement he serves as a professor and minister-at-large at Warner Southern College. *(see page 96)*

Forrest R. Robinson and his wife Peggy live in Lake Wales, Florida. Dr. Robinson has pastored for thirty-two years serving six churches. He was president of Mid-America Bible College in Oklahoma City and served as Interim General Director of Church of God Ministries. *(see page 88)*

David L. Sebastian and his wife Debbie live in Anderson, Indiana. Dr. Sebastian has been the Dean of the Anderson University School of Theology since 1995. He has pastored in Arizona and Ohio. *(see page 42)*

Frederick G. Shackleton and his wife Doris live in Murrieta, California. Dr. Shackleton has pastored five congregations and has taught at Anderson University, Warner Pacific College and Azusa Pacific University. He has written hymns, church school curriculum, and the book, *Toward a Living Hope. (see page 163)*

Fredrick H. Shively and his wife Kay live in Anderson, Indiana. Dr. Shively is a Professor of Bible and Religion at Anderson University. He has pastored congregations in California and Oregon. *(see page 185)*

Kay Murphy Shively and her husband Fred live in Anderson, Indiana. Kay is a writer, a former teacher and former program coordinator for WOMEN OF THE CHURCH OF GOD. She now works for Church of God Ministries in Global Missions as recuitment specialist and liaison to special assignment missionaries. *(see page 200)*

Risë Wood Singer and her husband David live in Pendleton, Indiana. She is retired after having worked in the legal field. *(see page 140)*

Janetta Hitt Slattery lives in Anderson, Indiana. She is a high school English teacher. *(see page 235)*

Billie Roy Smith lives in Huntsville, Alabama. He is an ordained minister, a writer and a retired Certified Public Accountant. *(see page 104)*

Margaret Jones Smith lives at Penney Farms in Florida. She is the former Editor of *Church of God MISSIONS. (see page 30)*

Nathan L. Smith and his wife Ann live in Anderson, Indiana. He is a former missionary to Japan and Korea. *(see page 180)*

Roscoe Snowden and his wife Nellie live in Anderson, Indiana. Dr. Snowden has pastored churches in North Carolina, Kentucky, Ohio, Alabama and Indiana. He was the Director of Church Service for the Church of God. After retirement he worked for fifteen years with World Service in the Department of Wills and Estate Planning. *(see page 50)*

Leonard W. Snyder and his wife Jean live in Delaware, Ohio. Dr. Snyder was Ohio State Coordinator for the Church of God. He pastored in North Carolina and Hamilton, Ohio, serving the Hamilton Church for thirty-three years. *(see page 154)*

James L. Sparks and his wife Susan live in Battle Creek, Michigan. He is Senior Pastor of North Avenue Church of God. *(see page 178)*

Gilbert W. Stafford and his wife Darlene live in Anderson, Indiana. Dr. Stafford is a former speaker for the Christian Brotherhood Hour. He is Professor of Christian Theology at Anderson University School of Theology. He is the author of the books *Church of God at the Crossroads* and *Vision for the Church of God at the Crossroads*. *(see page 208)*

Christie Smith Stephens and her husband Stan live in Anderson, Indiana. She is a writer and an advocate for survivors of domestic and sexual abuse/violence. Christie co-founded Women's Alternatives, Inc., a social service agency. She and David Liverett collaborated on the book *Oh, to be in Miss Collier's class again!* *(see pages 6, 39, 258, 280 and 302)*

R. Eugene Sterner lives in Anderson, Indiana. Dr. Sterner has pastored in Pennsylvania, Louisana, Alabama and Ohio. He is a former speaker for the Christian Brotherhood Hour. He has authored several books. *(see page 36)*

Merle D. Strege and his wife Fran live in Anderson, Indiana. Dr. Strege is a Professor of Bible and Religion at Anderson University. He has written several books and is the Church of God Historian. *(see page 80)*

Paul A. Tanner and his wife Jean live in Anderson, Indiana. Dr. Tanner is a former Director of World Service and was Executive Director of the Executive Council of the Church of God. *(see page 135)*

Gibb E. Webber and his wife Georgia live in Anderson, Indiana. He is a retired English professor at Anderson University. *(see page 45)*

William A. White and his wife Pam live in Anderson, Indiana. He is Adult Editor of *Bridges Curriculum* and the devotional booklet *Pathways to God*. *(see page 54)*

Richard L. Willowby and his wife Cheryl live in Anderson, Indiana. Richard is Senior Pastor at Hope Community Church of God in Clarksville, Indiana. He is the former Managing Editor of *Vital Christianity*. *(see page 86)*

Laura Benson Withrow and her husband Oral live in Anderson, Indiana. She is a writer of Church of God curriculum and has authored several books. *(see page 148)*

Amy Dudeck Witt lives in Anderson, Indiana. Amy was personal secretary to printing executives, F. G. Smith and Steele Smith at Warner Press in Anderson, Indiana, and an early elementary teacher and pastor's wife. *(see page 69)*

Gertrude E. Wunsch is retired and lives in Forestdale, Massachusetts, on Cape Cod. She was a Professor of Physical Education at Anderson University in Anderson, Indiana, for thirty-six years. *(see page 206)*

Churches

International Churches

Egypt
Page 130 - Maadi Community Church (1930), *Cairo, Egypt* - 57-EG

Isle of Man
Page 34 - Old Kirk Bradden (1774), *Isle of Man in the Irish Sea* - 12-IS

Japan
Page 192 - Tarumi Church of God (1967), *Kobe, Japan* - 92-JN
Page 176 - Hagiyama Church of God (1975), *Tokyo, Japan* - 88-JN
Page 181 - Tachikawa Church of God (1952), *Tokyo, Japan* - 76-JN
Page 173 - Tamagawa Church of God (1953), *Tokyo, Japan* - 36-JN

Lebanon
Page 112 - Ain Kfarzabad Church of God (1962), *Ain Kfarzabad, Lebanon* - 41-BL

Tanzania
Page 212 - Murray Church of God, *Mama Isara, Mbulu, Tanzania* - 87-TA

Matted prints may be purchased by using the identification number listed with each church.
(Example: 97AL idendifies *Old* Sixth Avenue Church of God in Decatur, Alabama).
Use the website for ordering instructions on all Chinaberry House products. www.2Lights.com
Chinaberry House, PO Box 505, Anderson, Indiana 46015 email: dliverett@aol.com

Epilogue

"'A little while, and you will no longer see me,
and again a little while, and you will see me.'"
—John 16:16

Roselawn Cemetery in Decatur, Alabama, is a place David Liverett and I know well. His parents, Monroe and Elna Liverett, are buried there just a few steps away from the graves of my Smith grandparents and my mother, Pearl Toon Smith. David and I have stood there with our families and friends to say farewell for now to those we love. Everyone who has written for this book has stood at a similar place feeling the ache of separation while holding on to the promises of scripture assuring us that this moment is not the end. We will see one another again. The circle will be unbroken by and by.

The journey didn't end in September of 1974, when we stood by her grave in Roselawn Cemetery and watched the red dirt fall upon her casket. The journey didn't end in June of 1975, nine months to the day of our last procession there, when we stood by his grave next to hers and watched the red dirt fall upon his casket. The life journeys of faith of Emma Elizabeth Means Smith and Marion Hickman Smith, my grandparents, didn't end with ashes to ashes and dust to dust. There is more to them than their physical bodies. They are spiritual presences living on and on. I can still hear my grandmama's laughter. I can still feel my granddaddy's arms around me.

The journey didn't end at Roselawn. Several years after we had gathered there my grandparents decided to come calling on me again. Some will say that it was only a dream and if it were not my experience I would likely agree with them. However, dreams and nightmares are filled and fraught with images strange most often very confusing. This was not the case when Grandmama and Granddaddy came to see me. I guess they knew how hard life had been, how abandoned by the church I felt, and they wanted to let me know that they and the church they loved were alive and well and loved me. There were three of them walking toward me, Grandmama, Granddaddy and a woman I did not recognize. She was shorter than my grandmother. It was Grandmama who spoke to me. "Christie, we want you to know that we are all right. We are over here now with Stella." That was it. Direct and to the point. I understood this message of love, reassurance and confirmation of faith but I didn't know who Stella was. A little while later I called my mom and dad to tell them of my *dream*. I asked, "Did Grandmama and Granddaddy know anyone named Stella and I don't mean Stella Standridge because she is still alive?" They couldn't think of anyone. We continued our conversation and then all of a sudden my mom said, "Well, there was Old Sister Stella Johnson but she's been dead for years!" My dad agreed.

Well, I'll probably not be able to prove that the visit was not just a dream until I cross Jordan and my faith is sight. But I know, as we say, beyond a shadow of a doubt, that my grandparents came to visit me to tell me that life is eternal. They brought their friend Stella Johnson with them so that I'd have to do a little research to verify some one whom I didn't already know. There was my granddaddy's question mark showing up again. I am sure that it was Grandmama's idea to come to see me and that she brought Granddaddy and Sister Johnson with her. My grandmother would never leave me and not find a way to tell me what she now knows. She always told me everything. She is a strong woman of faith. She lives. They live. They walk with me and talk with me.

I believe that David's folks and my folks and all those folks, loved by the writers and readers of this book, who have ended their walks of faith here are at the great Camp Meeting of The Spirit. Good News! The journey and the story never end. Brother Naylor was right, "Once again we come to the house of God..."

Emma Christie Smith Stephens

Acknowledgements

Saying Grace
Painting by Norman Rockwell, cover
Printed by permission of the Norman Rockwell Family Trust
Copyright ©1951 the Norman Rockwell Family Trust

Sunday Morning Meeting Time, page 48
©1995, 2002 Gaither Music Company, Inc. All rights reserved.
Used by permission of Gaither Copyright Management.

Generation to Generation — Celebrating the Teaching Church, page 71
A Song to the Glory of God. Dedicated to The Board of Christian Education
of the Church of God on the occasion of the 75th Anniversary.
Used by permission. Lyrics by Christie Smith Stephens
Music by Greg Gilpin
Copyright ©1998, Stephens and Gilpin

Scripture Selection, page 75
Eugene H. Peterson, *The Message*
(Colorado Springs: Navpress Publishing Group, 1995), 449.

I Am the Lord's, I Know, page 82
Used by permission. *Worship the Lord, Hymnal of the Church of God*
Copyright ©1989, Anderson, Indiana

The Church in the Wildwood, page 95
Public domain

I'll Follow with Rejoicing, page 131
Used by permission. *Worship the Lord, Hymnal of the Church of God*
Copyright ©1989, Anderson, Indiana

Consecration, page 210
Used by permission. *Worship the Lord, Hymnal of the Church of God*
Copyright ©1989, Anderson, Indiana

The Window Speaks, page 222
Used by permission. *Church of God Missions*, May/June 1996, page 4.
Esther Boyer Bauer

Dorothy Blevins Dicus, page 232
The retelling the faith journey story of her father, John A. Morrison.

Wholehearted Service, page 261
Used by permission. *Worship the Lord, Hymnal of the Church of God*
Copyright ©1989, Anderson, Indiana

Warner Sallman's Head of Christ, page 273
Used by permission. ©*Warner Press, Inc., Anderson, Indiana.*